INTRODUCTION TO
HADITH STUDIES

INTRODUCTION TO

HADITH STUDIES

BY **FURHAN ZUBAIRI**

Printed in the United States of America

First Publishing, 2019

ISBN: 9781793125187

Content input: Jawad Beg
Cover design, layout, and typesetting: Mohammad Bibi
Typeset in Lato, Nassim, Adobe Arabic, and
KFGQPC Uthmanic Script HAFS
Arabic Symbols: KFGQPC Arabic Symbols 01

Dedicated to my parents, family, and teachers.
May Allah continue to bless them and grant them
the highest ranks in Paradise.

CONTENTS

INTRODUCTION XVII

PRELIMINARY DEFINITIONS XXI

PART 1

CHAPTER 1 IMPORTANCE OF THE SUNNAH
- Explaining the Quran 3
- To follow the Sunnah is Mandatory 4
- Model Behavior/Role Model 7

CHAPTER 2 'ULUM AL-HADITH
- Definition 9
- Subject Matter 10
- Purpose 11
- Objective 11

CHAPTER 3 PRESERVATION & COMPILATION OF HADITH
- The Era of the Prophet ﷺ 14
- The Era of the Companions 22
- The Era of the Successors (Late 1st Century – Early 2nd Century) 23
- Compilation and Preservation in the Late 2nd Century 24
- Preservation and Compilation in the 3rd Century 26

CHAPTER 4
HADITH LITERATURE

al-Ṣaḥīfah 29
al-Muṣannaf 30
al-Musnad 30
al-Jāmiʿ 31
Sunan 32
al-Muʿjam 32
al-Mustadrak 33
al-Mustakhraj 33
al-Juzʾ 33
al-Sharḥ 33

CHAPTER 5
WELL-KNOWN HADITH WORKS & THEIR COMPILERS

Muwaṭṭaʾ of Imām Mālik ﵀ 35
Ṣaḥīḥ al-Bukhārī 36
Ṣaḥīḥ Muslim 38
Jāmiʿ of Imām al-Tirmidhi 39
Sunan Abī Dāwūd 41
Sunan al-Nasāʾī 42
Sunan ibn Mājah 42

CHAPTER 6
AL-ISNAD

Origins of the Isnād 46
The Expansion of the Isnād 47

CHAPTER 7
BIOGRAPHIES OF HADITH NARRATORS & CRITIQUE AND VALIDATION 49

PART 2

Classification of Ḥadīth 55

CHAPTER 8
CLASSIFICATION OF HADITH ACCORDING TO AUTHORITY

al-Ḥadīth al-Qudsī: The Divine Ḥadīth 58
al-Ḥadīth al-Marfūʿ: The Elevated Ḥadīth 60
al-Ḥadīth al-Mawqūf: The Suspended Ḥadīth 61
al-Ḥadīth al-Maqṭūʿ: The Severed (Cut-off) Ḥadīth 63

CHAPTER 9
CLASSIFICATION OF HADITH ACCORDING TO THE NUMBER OF NARRATORS

al-Ḥadīth al-Mutawātir: The Consecutively Recurrent Ḥadīth 66
Types of Mutawātir 67
Khabar al-Āḥād: The Solitary Report 70

CHAPTER 10
TYPES OF AHAD ACCORDING TO NUMBER OF NARRATORS

al-Mashhūr (The Well-Known) 74
al-ʿAzīz (The Strong Ḥadīth) 76
al-Gharīb (The Isolated Ḥadīth) 78

CHAPTER 11
CLASSIFICATION OF AHAD WITH RESPECT TO STRENGTH & WEAKNESS

al-Ṣaḥīḥ: The Authentic Ḥadīth 84
al-Ḥasan: The Fair Ḥadīth 87
al-Ṣaḥīḥ li Ghayrihi (The Extrinsically Authentic Ḥadīth) 88
al-Ḍaʿīf (The Weak Ḥadīth) 89
al-Ḥasan li Ghayrihi (The Extrinsically Fair Ḥadīth) 91

Transliteration & Pronunciation Key

Arabic Letter	Transliteration	Sound
ء	ʾ	A slight catch in the breath, cutting slightly short the preceding syllable.
ا	*ā*	An elongated *a* as in *cat*.
ب	*b*	As in *best*.
ت	*t*	As in *ten*.
ث	*th*	As in *thin*.
ج	*j*	As in *jewel*.
ح	*ḥ*	Tensely breathed *h* sound made by dropping tongue into back of throat, forcing the air out.
خ	*kh*	Pronounced like the *ch* in Scottish *loch*, made by touching back of tongue to roof of mouth and forcing air out.
د	*d*	As in *depth*.
ذ	*dh*	A thicker *th* sound as in *the*.
ر	*r*	A rolled *r*, similar to Spanish.
ز	*z*	As in *zest*.
س	*s*	As in *seen*.
ش	*sh*	As in *sheer*.
ص	*ṣ*	A heavy *s* pronounced far back in the mouth with the mouth hollowed to produce full sound.
ض	*ḍ*	A heavy *d/dh* pronounced far back in the mouth with the mouth hollowed to produce a full sound.
ط	*ṭ*	A heavy *t* pronounced far back in the mouth with the mouth hollowed to produce a full sound.
ظ	*ẓ*	A heavy *dh* pronounced far back in the mouth with the mouth hollowed to produce a full sound.
ع	ʿ	A guttural sound pronouned narrowing the throat.
غ	*gh*	Pronounced like a throaty French *r* with the mouth hallowed.
ف	*f*	As in *feel*.
ق	*q*	A guttural *q* sound made from the back of the throat with the mouth hallowed.
ك	*k*	As in *kit*.
ل	*l*	As in *lip*.
م	*m*	As in *melt*.
ن	*n*	As in *nest*.
ه	*h*	As in *hen*.

و	*w* (at the beg. of syllable)	As in *west*.
	ū (in the middle of syllable)	An elongated *oo* sound, as in *boo*.
ي	*y* (at beg. of syllable)	As in *yes*.
	ī (in the middle of syllable)	An elongated *ee* sound, as in *seen*.

سبحانه وتعالى Used following the mention of Allah, God, translated as, "Glorified and Exalted be He."

ﷺ Used following the mention of the Prophet Muḥammad, translated as, "May God honor and protect him."

عليه السلام Used following the mention of any other prophet or Gabriel, translated as, "May God's protection be upon him."

رضي الله عنهم Used following the mention of the Prophet Muḥammad's Companions, translated as, "May God be pleased with them."

رضي الله عنه Used following the mention of a male Companion of the Prophet Muḥammad, translated as, "May God be pleased with him."

رضي الله عنها Used following the mention of a female Companion of the Prophet Muḥammad, translated as, "May God be pleased with her."

رضي الله عنهما Used following the mention of two Companions of the Prophet Muḥammad, translated as, "May God be pleased with them both."

رحمهم الله Used following the mention of the major scholars of Islam, translated as, "May God have mercy on them."

رحمه الله Used following the mention of a major scholar of Islam, translated as, "May God have mercy on him."

INTRODUCTION
FROM THE AUTHOR

In the name of Allah the Most Merciful,
the Very Merciful.

All thanks and praise are due to Allah ﷻ, the Lord of the worlds, and may His peace and blessings be upon His last and final messenger, Muḥammad ﷺ, his family, his Companions, and those who follow them until the end of times.

Among Islamic disciplines, Ḥadīth Studies have a unique and special status. This branch of knowledge is considered to be one of the most noble Islamic Sciences. A topic's distinction is directly related to the honor and distinction of its subject matter. What greater honor and distrinction then to be connected to Allah's messenger? Regarding this concept, Imām al-Nawawī ﵀ writes, "The science of ḥadīth is the noblest means for attaining closeness to the Lord of the Worlds. How can it not be so, when it is the exposition of the way of the best of mankind and the most noble of the first and last of creation: Muḥammad ﷺ?"

The reason why Ḥadīth Studies is so special is because it is the study of the words, actions, approvals, and characteristics of the last and final Messenger, the leader of the Prophets, the most noble human being to walk on the face of this Earth, our beloved Muḥammad ﷺ. Our teachers would say that it is an honor and privilege for us to be given the opportunity to study anything related to the aḥādīth [plural of ḥadīth] of the Prophet ﷺ.

The importance of aḥādīth and the Sunnah within the framework of Islam cannot be overemphasized; they are foundational to our belief and practice. There are two primary sources of Islam: the Quran and Sunnah. Broadly speaking, the Quran provides us with general rules, principles, morals, values, ethics, and ideas while the Sunnah provides the details. In other words, the Sunnah of the Prophet ﷺ is a detailed explanation of what is mentioned by Allah ﷻ in the Quran. It is impossible to act upon the Quran, to follow its guidance, teachings, commands, and prohibitions without the Sunnah of the Prophet ﷺ.

It is narrated that once ʿImrān ibn Ḥuṣayn رضي الله عنه was sitting with his students when a man came and said, "Do not speak to us except with the Quran." ʿImrān asked him to come close and said, "Tell me, if you and your companions relied upon the Quran alone, would you find that ẓuhr prayer is four units, ʿaṣr is four units, maghrib is three units, and that you have to recite in the first two units? Tell me, if you and your companions relied upon the Quran alone, would you find that ṭawāf is seven circuits and that walking between Ṣafā and Marwah is seven circuits? O people! Take (the Sunnah) from us, because, by Allah, if you do not, you will go astray."[1]

This incident highlights just one aspect of the importance of the Sunnah. Without it, we would have no practical way of implementing the Quran. We would not know how to worship Allah ﷻ properly. Imām Abū Ḥanīfah رحمه الله said, "Had it not been for the Sunnah, none of us would have understood the Quran." Imām al-Shāfiʿī رحمه الله said, "Everything the imams say is an explanation of the Sunnah, and the entire Sunnah is an explanation of the Quran."

Alḥamdulillāh, through the grace and mercy of Allah ﷻ, I have been blessed with the opportunity to develop and teach a course through IOK Extension, which is now the Part-Time Seminary, on the Sciences of Ḥadīth. While preparing for the course, I compiled a set of personal notes that I would use to teach the class. The course is also taught to the IOK Seminary students before they begin their study of ḥadīth. I thought that it would be beneficial for our students, as well as other students of knowledge, to compile my notes into a short booklet that can serve as a brief introduction to the Sciences of Ḥadīth in order to help establish a basic level of literacy within the subject.

---

1 al-Bayhaqī, *Madkhal al-Dalāʾil*

INTRODUCTION

The purpose of this booklet is to provide, what I consider to be, something similar to "cliff notes" for Ḥadīth Studies.

I compiled the notes primarily from five sources:

1. *A Textbook of Ḥadīth Studies* by Professor Hashim Kamali
2. *Studies in Ḥadīth Methodology and Literature* by Dr. Muhammad Mustafa Azami
3. *Hadith: Muhammad's Legacy in the Medieval and Modern World* by Dr. Jonathan Brown
4. *Manhaj al-Naqd fī ʿUlūm al-Ḥadīth* by the eminent scholar Nūr al-Dīn ʿIṭr
5. *Taysīr Muṣṭalaḥ al-Ḥadīth* by the teacher of one of my teachers Dr. Maḥmūd al-Ṭaḥḥān.

This is not an original work; rather, it is a summary of what I found to be beneficial and important for beginning students of knowledge or for those interested in having a solid introduction to the study of ḥadīth.

I would like to thank all of those individuals who provided suggestions, comments, improvements and took the time out of their busy schedules to edit this short work. May Allah ﷻ reward our IOK Seminary students Mudassir Mayet and Ayesha Hussain, as well as Shaykh Joe Bradford, continue to bless them, and increase them in knowledge.

I ask Allah ﷻ to bless this small effort and make it beneficial for those who read it. I ask Allah ﷻ to bless all of us with a deep appreciation for the entire field of Ḥadīth Studies and to increase our love for the Prophet ﷺ. May Allah shower His blessings and mercy upon His last and final messenger, Muḥammad ﷺ.

Furhan Zubairi
Diamond Bar, CA
November 3, 2018 / Ṣafar 25, 1440

PRELIMINARY DEFINITIONS

AL-ḤADĪTH (THE NARRATION)

Linguistically, the word ḥadīth means something new, the opposite of something old.

الجديد، ضد القديم

Technically, the word ḥadīth refers to a statement, action, or tacit approval attributed to the Prophet ﷺ. Similarly, it is sometimes also used to refer to a statement, action, or tacit approval of a Companion ﵁ or even a Successor ﵀.

ما أضيف إلى النبي ﷺ من قول أو فعل أو تقرير أو صفة

AL-KHABAR (REPORT)

Linguistically, the word khabar means news or information.

النبأ

Technically, it is used to refer to what has been narrated from the Prophet ﷺ or someone other than him.

ما جاء عن النبي ﷺ أو عن غيره

So the word khabar is more general than the word ḥadīth; every ḥadīth is a khabar but not every khabar is necessarily a ḥadīth. Generally speaking, ḥadīth scholars use it as a synonym for ḥadīth.

AL-ATHAR (TRADITION)

Linguistically, the word athar means trace or effect.

بقية الشيء

Technically, it is used to refer to a statement, action, or tacit approval attributed to a Companion ﷺ.

ما أضيف إلى الصحابة من أقوال وأفعال

It is also sometimes used as a synonym for the word ḥadīth. For example, Imam al-Ṭaḥāwī ﷺ entitled his famous work *Sharḥ Maʿānī al-Āthār* even though it includes narrations attributed to the Prophet ﷺ.

AL-SUNNAH (THE WAY)

Linguistically, the word sunnah means a way or usual path, regardless of whether it is good or bad.

السيرة والطريقة المعتادة حسنة كانت أو قبيحة

Technically, the word sunnah can have different meanings depending on who is using it and in what context it is being used. In the most general sense, it refers to the way of the Prophet ﷺ in everything he did, regardless of whether that action is legally considered to be obligatory (farḍ), mandatory (wājib), or recommended (mustaḥabb).

الطريقة المشروعة المتبعة فى الدين، والمنهج النبوى الحنيف

According to the jurists, it is a legal value assigned to a person's actions. If a person does it, then they will be rewarded. If they leave it, then there is no blame upon them. The jurists define it as something that the Prophet ﷺ did on a regular and consistent basis as an act of devotion, while leaving it sometimes without an excuse.

ما واظب عليه النبى ﷺ على وجه العبادة، مع الترك أحيانا
لغير عذر

As for the scholars of ḥadīth, they use it as a synonym for the word ḥadīth.

PART 1:

OVERVIEW OF HADITH STUDIES

1

IMPORTANCE OF THE SUNNAH

As mentioned in the introduction, the importance of aḥādīth and the Sunnah within the framework of Islam cannot be overemphasized; they are a foundational aspect of belief and practice. There are two primary sources of Islam: the Quran and Sunnah. Broadly speaking, the Quran provides general rules, principles, morals, values, ethics and ideals while the Sunnah provides the details. In other words, the Sunnah of the Prophet ﷺ is a detailed explanation of what is mentioned by Allah ﷻ in the Quran. It is impossible to act upon the Quran, to follow its guidance, teachings, commands, and prohibitions without the Sunnah of the Prophet ﷺ. There are a number of reasons why the Sunnah is considered to be central to Islamic beliefs and practices and several articles and booklets have been written on this topic.

EXPLAINING THE QURAN

Allah ﷻ revealed the noble Quran as a book of guidance illuminating the path towards happiness and success both in this world and the next. Allah ﷻ gave the Quran to the Prophet ﷺ as an everlasting miracle, whose miraculous nature can be seen and experienced until the end of time. Along with the Quran, Allah ﷻ gave the Prophet ﷺ the Sunnah as a detailed explanation of what is in the Quran.

Allah ﷻ says, “And We revealed to you the message that you may make clear to the people what was sent down to them and that they might give thought.”[1]

وَأَنزَلْنَا إِلَيْكَ الذِّكْرَ لِتُبَيِّنَ لِلنَّاسِ مَا نُزِّلَ إِلَيْهِمْ وَلَعَلَّهُمْ يَتَفَكَّرُونَ

Allah ﷻ also says, “And We have not revealed to you the Book, [O Muḥammad], except for you to make clear to them that wherein they have differed and as guidance and mercy for a people who believe.”[2]

وَمَا أَنزَلْنَا عَلَيْكَ الْكِتَابَ إِلَّا لِتُبَيِّنَ لَهُمُ الَّذِى اخْتَلَفُوا فِيهِ ۙ وَهُدًى
وَرَحْمَةً لِّقَوْمٍ يُؤْمِنُونَ

In these two verses and several others throughout the Quran, Allah ﷻ is explicitly stating that one of the responsibilities of the Prophet ﷺ was to explain the book of Allah. In other words, the Sunnah of the Prophet ﷺ is a detailed explanation of what is mentioned by Allah ﷻ in the Quran. To reiterate, it is impossible to act upon the Quran, to follow the guidance, teachings, commands, and prohibitions without the Sunnah of the Prophet ﷺ.

TO FOLLOW THE SUNNAH IS MANDATORY

In addition to that there are numerous verses that make it explicitly clear that it is obligatory to follow the Sunnah of the Prophet ﷺ. In several places throughout the Quran Allah ﷻ makes it an obligation to obey His messenger and follow him.

“O you who have believed, obey Allah and obey the Messenger and those in authority among you. And if you disagree over anything, refer it to Allah and the Messenger, if you should believe in Allah and the Last Day. That is the best [way] and best in result.”[3]

1 Quran, 16:44
2 Quran, 16:64
3 Quran, 4:59

يَا أَيُّهَا الَّذِينَ آمَنُوا أَطِيعُوا اللَّهَ وَأَطِيعُوا الرَّسُولَ وَأُولِي الْأَمْرِ مِنكُمْ
ۖ فَإِن تَنَازَعْتُمْ فِي شَيْءٍ فَرُدُّوهُ إِلَى اللَّهِ وَالرَّسُولِ إِن كُنتُمْ تُؤْمِنُونَ
بِاللَّهِ وَالْيَوْمِ الْآخِرِ ۚ ذَٰلِكَ خَيْرٌ وَأَحْسَنُ تَأْوِيلًا

"He who obeys the Messenger has obeyed Allah; but those who turn away - We have not sent you over them as a guardian."[4]

مَّن يُطِعِ الرَّسُولَ فَقَدْ أَطَاعَ اللَّهَ ۖ وَمَن تَوَلَّىٰ فَمَا أَرْسَلْنَاكَ
عَلَيْهِمْ حَفِيظًا

"It is not for a believing man or a believing woman, when Allah and His Messenger have decided a matter, that they should [thereafter] have any choice about their affair. And whoever disobeys Allah and His Messenger has certainly strayed into clear error."[5]

وَمَا كَانَ لِمُؤْمِنٍ وَلَا مُؤْمِنَةٍ إِذَا قَضَى اللَّهُ وَرَسُولُهُ أَمْرًا أَن يَكُونَ
لَهُمُ الْخِيَرَةُ مِنْ أَمْرِهِمْ ۗ وَمَن يَعْصِ اللَّهَ وَرَسُولَهُ فَقَدْ ضَلَّ
ضَلَالًا مُّبِينًا

"And whatever the Messenger has given you - take; and what he has forbidden you - refrain from. And fear Allah; indeed, Allah is severe in penalty."[6]

وَمَا آتَاكُمُ الرَّسُولُ فَخُذُوهُ وَمَا نَهَاكُمْ عَنْهُ فَانتَهُوا ۚ وَاتَّقُوا اللَّهَ ۖ
إِنَّ اللَّهَ شَدِيدُ الْعِقَابِ

"Say, [O Muḥammad], "If you should love Allah, then follow me, [so] Allah will love you and forgive you your sins. And Allah is Forgiving and

4 Quran, 4:80

5 Quran, 33:36

6 Quran, 59:7

Merciful."[7]

قُلْ إِن كُنتُمْ تُحِبُّونَ اللَّهَ فَاتَّبِعُونِي يُحْبِبْكُمُ اللَّهُ وَيَغْفِرْ لَكُمْ
ذُنُوبَكُمْ ۗ وَاللَّهُ غَفُورٌ رَّحِيمٌ

The claim that following the Sunnah is not necessary or that the aḥādīth are unreliable is absolutely ridiculous.

Similarly, there are a number of narrations from the Prophet ﷺ that talk about the importance of holding on to his guidance in every single thing, whether big or small, significant or insignificant.

The Prophet ﷺ said, "So you must keep to my sunnah and to the sunnah of the Khulafāʾ al-Rāshidūn (the Rightly Guided Caliphs), those who guide to the correct way. Cling to it stubbornly [literally: with your molar teeth]. Beware of newly invented matters [in the religion], for verily every innovation (bidʿah) is misguidance."[8]

فَعَلَيْكُم بِسُنَّتِي وَسُنَّةِ الْخُلَفَاءِ الرَّاشِدِينَ الْمَهْدِيِّينَ، عَضُّوا عَلَيْهَا
بِالنَّوَاجِذِ وَإِيَّاكُم وَمُحْدَثَاتِ الأُمُورِ؛ فَإِنَّ كُلَّ بِدعَةٍ ضَلَالَةٌ

The Prophet ﷺ said, "To proceed, the best speech is the Book of Allah and the best guidance is the guidance of Muhammad ﷺ, the worst practice is the introduction of new practices in Islam and every innovation [in religion] is a misguidance."[9]

أَمَّا بَعدُ؛ فَإِنَّ خَيرَ الْحَدِيثِ كِتَابُ اللَّهِ وَخَيرَ الْهَدِى هَدىُ مُحَمَّدٍ،
صَلَّى اللَّهُ عَلَيهِ وَسَلَّمَ، وَشَرَّ الأُمُورِ مُحدَثَاتُهَا، وَكُلُّ بِدعَةٍ ضَلَالَةٌ

There are also multiple narrations that encourage reviving and following the Sunnah of the Prophet ﷺ. Narrations that talk about the blessings, rewards, and virtues of following in the footsteps of the Prophet ﷺ.

The Prophet ﷺ said, "'Whoever revives a Sunnah of mine that dies out

7 Quran, 3:31

8 Abū Dāwūd, *k. al-sunnah, b. fī luzūm al-sunnah*, 4607

9 Muslim, *k. al-jumuʿah, b. takhfīf al-ṣalah wa al-khuṭbah*, 867

after I am gone, he will have a reward equivalent to that of those among the people who act upon it, without that detracting from their reward in the slightest."[10]

مَن أَحيَا سُنَّةً مِن سُنَّتِي قَد أُمِيتَت بَعدِى فَإِنَّ لَهُ مِنَ الأَجرِ مِثلَ أَجرِ مَن عَمِلَ بِهَا مِنَ النَّاسِ لاَ يَنقُصُ مِن أُجُورِ النَّاسِ شَيئًا

The Prophet ﷺ said, "The one who holds on tightly to my Sunnah when corruption in my nation spreads, for him the reward of a hundred martyrs."[11]

المُتَمَسِكُ بِسُنَّتِي عِندَ فَسَادِ أُمَّتِي لَهُ أَجرُ مِائَةِ شَهِيدٍ

MODEL BEHAVIOR/ROLE MODEL

Allah ﷻ says, "Indeed in the Messenger of Allah you have a good example to follow for him who hopes in Allah and the Last Day and remembers Allah much."[12]

لَّقَدْ كَانَ لَكُمْ فِي رَسُولِ اللَّهِ أُسْوَةٌ حَسَنَةٌ لِّمَن كَانَ يَرْجُو اللَّهَ وَالْيَوْمَ الْآخِرَ وَذَكَرَ اللَّهَ كَثِيرًا

The Prophet ﷺ is the ideal role model for believers to follow in every single aspect of their lives; personal, social, communal, economic, and political. The Prophet ﷺ was a physical manifestation of the teachings of the Quran; his life was built upon the beliefs, morals, values, and principles mentioned in the Quran. That is why when his wife ʿĀ'ishah ﷺ was asked regarding his character she replied, "His character was the Quran."[13] The Prophet ﷺ had the most noble character and manners; he was extremely kind, gentle, caring, friendly, affable, generous, compassionate, patient,

10 al-Tirmidhī, *k. al-ʿilm ʿan rasūlillah* ﷺ, *b. mā jā'a fī al-akdh bi al-sunnah wa ijtināb al-bidaʿi*, 2677

11 al-Haythamī, *Majmaʿ al-Zawā'id*, 177

12 Quran, 33:21

13 al-Bukhārī, *al-Adab al-Mufrad*, 308

forbearing, forgiving, brave, humble, and simple. He dealt with people in the most beautiful way possible. Allah ﷻ praises him in the Quran saying, "And you are surely on an excellent standard of character."[14]

That is why scholars of hadīth are seen in every single generation striving, struggling, and giving importance to preserving and reviving the Sunnah of the Prophet ﷺ. It is through their tireless efforts that almost every single aspect of the life of the Prophet ﷺ has been preserved. This effort started with the Companions of the Prophet ﷺ and continues till this day.

14 Quran, 68:4

2

‘ULUM AL-HADITH

THE SCIENCES OF HADITH

Before approaching the study of any discipline, it is part of the Islamic scholarly tradition to first discuss a few preliminary remarks regarding that discipline. These preliminary remarks are called the mabādiʾ, which are the definition, subject matter, purpose, and objective of the discipline itself. The mabādiʾ allow a student to approach the subject with a very basic understanding and outline of what is going to be studied.

DEFINITION

ʿUlūm al-Ḥadīth is a compound phrase made up of two words: ʿulūm and al-ḥadīth. ʿUlūm is the plural of the word ʿilm, which is usually translated as knowledge or science. In this context, it is referring to the studies associated with a specific subject matter. The word ḥadīth is used to refer to a statement, action, tacit approval, or characteristic attributed to the Prophet ﷺ. ʿUlūm al-Ḥadīth can thus be translated as Ḥadīth Studies or the Sciences of Ḥadīth.

ʿUlūm al-Ḥadīth is a branch of knowledge that deals with the study of the sayings, actions, tacit approvals, and characteristics of the Prophet ﷺ in terms of their transmission and understanding. Transmission refers to how these reports were passed on from generation to generation, both orally as well as through writing. Understanding refers to what lessons, morals, and rules can be extracted from the narrations. There are two main branches of ʿUlūm al-Ḥadīth:

1. ʿilm riwāyah al-ḥadīth (علم رواية الحديث)
2. ʿilm dirāyah al-ḥadīth (علم دراية الحديث)

ʿIlm riwāyah al-ḥadīth, knowledge of ḥadīth transmission, deals with the actual preservation, transmission, reporting, and narration of ḥadīth. This is the aspect of Ḥadīth Studies that focuses on the various classifications of ḥadīth, such as according to the number of narrators, according to how it was transmitted, according to who said it, according to acceptance and non-acceptance, according to continuity of the chain, according to breaks in the chain, etc. It has been defined as the branch of knowledge through which the reality of the narration, its conditions, how it is connected or broken, and the conditions of the narrators are known.[15] It analyzes the chain and its narrators to determine the authenticity of the narration. It is through this branch of knowledge that the ḥadīth of the Prophet ﷺ have been preserved and safeguarded from any alterations and fabrications. It is also known as Uṣūl al-Ḥadīth and Muṣṭalaḥ al-Ḥadīth (Ḥadīth Terminology). It played a major role in the preservation of Islam. This branch of knowledge is also something that is unique to Islam. It is a unique contribution to the social sciences for preserving and verifying any reports attributed to the Prophet ﷺ. No other religion has developed anything as complex or sophisticated.

ʿIlm dirāyah al-ḥadīth, knowledge of understanding ḥadīth, deals with understanding the meanings of the ḥadīth: what do the words themselves mean, what are the intended meanings, what lessons, morals, guidance, and rulings can be understood from them, etc.[16] In other words, this branch of Ḥadīth Studies deals with understanding the actual text itself.

SUBJECT MATTER

The subject matter is primarily two things, which are the two components of every ḥadīth:

---

15 هو علم يعرف به حقيقة الرواية و شروطها و كيفية الاتصال و الانقطاع و حال الرواة و ما يتصل بذلك

16 هو علم يبحث فيه عن المعنى المفهوم من ألفاظ الحديث و عن المعنى المراد منها مبنيا على قواعد العربية و ضوابط الشرعية و مطابقا لأحوال النبي صلى الله عليه وسلم

1. the chain of transmission (sanad)
2. the text (matn) of the ḥadīth

The sanad is the chain of narrators that connects the narrators of the ḥadīth, such as al-Bukhārī ﷺ, back to the Prophet ﷺ. **The matn** is the actual text of the narration.

Example:

حَدَّثَنَا سُلَيْمَانُ أَبُو الرَّبِيعِ، قَالَ حَدَّثَنَا إِسْمَاعِيلُ بْنُ جَعْفَرٍ، قَالَ حَدَّثَنَا نَافِعُ بْنُ مَالِكِ بْنِ أَبِي عَامِرٍ أَبُو سُهَيْلٍ، عَنْ أَبِيهِ، عَنْ أَبِي هُرَيْرَةَ، عَنِ النَّبِيِّ صلى الله عليه وسلم قَالَ: "آيَةُ الْمُنَافِقِ ثَلاَثٌ إِذَا حَدَّثَ كَذَبَ، وَإِذَا وَعَدَ أَخْلَفَ، وَإِذَا اؤْتُمِنَ خَانَ"[17]

The sanad of this ḥadīth is: Imām al-Bukhārī said that Sulaymān Abū al-Rabīʿ narrated to us, who said that Ismāʿīl ibn Jaʿfar narrated to us, who said that Nāfiʿ ibn Mālik ibn Abī ʿĀmir Abū Suhayl narrated to us, from his father, from Abū Hurayrah, from the Prophet ﷺ who said: "The signs of a hypocrite are three: whenever he speaks he lies, whenever he makes a promise he breaks it, and whenever he is trusted with something he breaks the trust."[18]

PURPOSE

The purpose of studying ʿUlūm al-Ḥadīth is to understand and appreciate the transmission, preservation, and proper understanding of the aḥādīth of the Prophet ﷺ.

OBJECTIVE

The main objective behind studying any Islamic Science is to attain the pleasure of Allah ﷻ in order to be successful in this life and the next.

---

17 The sanad (chain) is in grey and the matn (text) is in black.

18 al-Bukhārī, *k. al-adab, b. qawlillah yā ayuha allathīna āmanū ittaqu Allah wa kūnū maʿ al-ṣādiqīn*, 6095

3

PRESERVATION & COMPILATION OF HADITH

The Quran is the only revealed scripture that has been guaranteed protection by Allah ﷻ. Allah ﷻ Himself took the responsibility of preserving the Quran. He says, "Indeed, it is We who sent down the Remembrance and indeed, We will be its guardian."[19] Allah ﷻ has promised to protect the Quran from any distortions, discrepancies, and additions or deletions. This divine protection extends to the aḥādīth of the Prophet ﷺ as well. That is why there have been efforts to preserve and record the Prophet's narrations since the earliest days of Islam until today. The care and attention to minute details given in the preservation and compilation of ḥadīth is unparalleled.

The preservation and compilation of ḥadīth passed through four primary stages:

1. the life of the Prophet ﷺ
2. the era of the Companions رضي الله عنهم
3. the era of the Successors رحمهم الله
4. the era of structured or formal compilation

19 Quran 15:9

THE ERA OF THE PROPHET ﷺ

During the life of the Prophet ﷺ, the learning and teaching of aḥādīth was highly encouraged. The Prophet ﷺ employed multiple methods to ensure that his teachings were learned, preserved, and passed on, such as establishing informal schools and providing encouragement and motivation by mentioning the virtues, rewards, and blessings associated with learning.

The Prophet ﷺ established a number of informal schools throughout Madīnah and wherever else he ﷺ would send his Companions to teach. For example, before migration, the Prophet ﷺ sent Muṣʿab ibn ʿUmayr and Ibn Umm Maktūm رضي الله عنهما to Madīnah as teachers. After arriving in Madīnah, one of the first things the Prophet ﷺ did was establish his mosque, which served as an informal school. He also appointed one of his Companions, ʿAbdullāh ibn Saʿīd ibn al-ʿĀṣ رضي الله عنه, to teach people how to write. Oftentimes when delegations would come to Madīnah, he ﷺ would appoint a certain Companion to teach them the details of Islam. Similarly, the Prophet ﷺ sent a number of his Companions رضي الله عنهم to other places where people had become Muslim to teach them their religion. All of this created an environment of learning and teaching the sunnah of the Prophet ﷺ.

The Prophet ﷺ also encouraged his Companions to learn and preserve his teachings. There are numerous narrations from the Prophet ﷺ that encouraged the companions to learn and teach ḥadīth by mentioning its rewards, virtues, and blessings. The following are a few examples:

- The Messenger of Allah ﷺ said: "May Allah cause a slave (of His) to flourish, the one who hears my words and understands them, then he conveys them from me. There are those who have knowledge but lack understanding, and there may be those who convey knowledge to those who may have more understanding than they do."[20]

نَضَّرَ اللَّهُ عَبدًا سَمِعَ مَقَالَتِي فَوَعَاهَا ثُمَّ بَلَّغَهَا عَنِّي فَرُبَّ
حَامِلِ فِقهٍ غَيرِ فَقِيهٍ وَرُبَّ حَامِلِ فِقهٍ إِلَى مَن هُوَ أَفقَهُ مِنهُ

- The Prophet ﷺ said, "Convey from me, even if it is one verse of the

20 Ibn Mājah, *k. al-Muqaddimah*, 242

Quran..."[21]

$$\text{بَلِّغُوا عَنِّي وَلَوْ آيَةً}$$

- The Messenger of Allah ﷺ delivered a sermon on the Day of Slaughter said: "Let those who are present convey to those who are absent. Maybe the one to whom it is conveyed to will understand it better than the one who (first) heard it."[22]

$$\text{خَطَبَ رَسُولُ اللَّهِ ـ صَلَّى اللَّهُ عَلَيْهِ وَسَلَّمَ ـ يَوْمَ النَّحْرِ فَقَالَ:}$$
$$\text{"لِيُبَلِّغِ الشَّاهِدُ الغَائِبَ فَإِنَّهُ رُبَّ مُبَلَّغٍ يُبَلِّغُهُ أَوْعَى لَهُ مِن سَامِعٍ"}$$

- Ibn 'Abbās ؓ narrated that the Prophet ﷺ said, "O Allah! Have mercy upon my successors." We said, "And who are your successors, O Messenger of Allah?" He said, "Those who narrate my ḥadīth and teach them to the people."[23]

$$\text{"اللَّهُمَّ ارْحَمْ خُلَفَائِي!" قُلْنَا: وَمَنْ خُلَفَاؤُكَ يَا رَسُولَ اللهِ؟}$$
$$\text{قَالَ: "الَّذِينَ يَرْوُونَ أَحَادِيثِي وَ يُعَلِّمُونَهَا النَّاسَ"}$$

The Prophet ﷺ also encouraged his Companions ؓ to learn and teach by mentioning the numerous rewards, blessings, and virtues associated with the noble acts of learning and teaching. The following are just a few examples:

- The Prophet ﷺ said, "Seeking knowledge is an obligation on every single Muslim."[24]

$$\text{طَلَبُ العِلْمِ فَرِيضَةٌ عَلَى كُلِّ مُسْلِمٍ}$$

---

[21] al-Bukhārī, k. aḥadīth al-anbiyāʾ, b. mā dhukira ʿan banī isrāʾīl, 3461
[22] Ibn Mājah, k. al-muqaddimah, 239
[23] al-Mundhirī, al-Targhīb wa al-Tarhīb, 87
[24] Ibn Mājah, k. al-Muqaddimah, 229

- "Whoever travels a path seeking knowledge, Allah ﷻ makes the path to Paradise easy for them."[25]

مَن سَلَكَ طَرِيقًا يَلتَمِسُ فِيهِ عِلمًا سَهَّلَ اللَّهُ لَهُ طَرِيقًا إِلَى الجَنَّةِ

- "Whoever travels a path seeking knowledge is in the path of Allah ﷻ until they return."[26]

مَن خَرَجَ فِي طَلَبِ العِلمِ فَهُوَ فِي سَبِيلِ اللَّهِ حَتَّى يَرجِعَ

TEACHING METHODS OF THE PROPHET ﷺ

One of the many roles of the Prophet ﷺ was that of a teacher, and as a teacher he employed several different methods of teaching. The Prophet ﷺ ensured that his Sunnah would be preserved using three primary methods of teaching:

1. speaking
2. practical demonstration
3. writing

1. VERBAL TEACHING

This was the most widespread and common method of teaching during the time of the Prophet ﷺ. There were numerous Companions of the Prophet ﷺ who were engaged in learning, memorizing, and teaching aḥādīth. These individuals were gifted with amazing memories. An average person would have thousands of lines of poetry memorized. A number of people would have their own lineages memorized along with the lineages of their horses. The Arabs had a very strong oral tradition of poetry and storytelling that enhanced their ability to memorize.

---

25 al-Tirmidhī, *k. al-ʿilm ʿan rasūl Allah* ﷺ, *b. mā jāʾ fī fadl talab al-ʿilm*, 2646

26 al-Tirmidhī, *k. al-ʿilm ʿan rasūl Allah* ﷺ, *b. mā jāʾ fī fadl talab al-ʿilm*, 2647

There is an amazing incident narrated regarding the unique memory of Abū Hurayrah ؓ. Once the governor of Madīnah, Marwān ibn al-Ḥakam, wanted to test Abū Hurayrah's memory to see how strong it really was and how accurate he was in narrating ḥadīth. So he invited Abū Hurayrah ؓ and asked him to narrate a number of aḥādīth. He asked a scribe to hide behind a curtain and write down whatever Abū Hurayrah ؓ narrated. Then a year later he invited him again and asked him to narrate the exact same aḥādīth he had narrated the year before. Marwān again had the scribe hide behind the curtain and write down everything Abū Hurayrah ؓ narrated. Afterwards, they compared the two dictations and found that they were exactly the same! Not a single word was added, deleted, or changed around.

It is no surprise or shock that the Companions would memorize the exact words of the Prophet ﷺ, given that he encouraged them to do so. They used to listen to every single word of the Prophet ﷺ with the utmost care and attention. They used to learn both the Quran and ḥadīth from the Prophet ﷺ, mostly in the Prophet's mosque. When the Prophet ﷺ would step out, they would review amongst themselves. Anas ؓ narrated, "We sat with the Prophet ﷺ, maybe sixty people in number, and the Prophet ﷺ taught us ḥadīth. Later, when he went out for any need, we used to memorize it amongst ourselves. When we left, it was as if we had cultivated it in our hearts."[27]

Also, when the Prophet ﷺ would speak, he would speak clearly and audibly, often repeating important things thrice. Oftentimes he would listen to what the Companions ؓ had learned. Even the Companions who were unable to attend these gatherings would learn the aḥadīth from those who were present. ʿUmar ؓ narrated, "A neighbor of mine and I used to take turns attending sessions with the Messenger of Allah ﷺ. He would attend one day and I would the next, and then we informed one another of the events of that day and any new revelation that might have been communicated."[28]

2. *PRACTICAL DEMONSTRATION*

Another way in which the Companions learned and taught ḥadīth was through practical demonstration. Oftentimes, the Prophet ﷺ would do something and tell the Companions ؓ to do it the same way. For example,

27 al-Khaṭīb, *al-Jāmi⊠*, 43a

28 al-Bukhārī, *k. al-nikāh, b. mawʾidhah al-rajul ibnatahu lihāl zawjihā*, 5191

the Prophet ﷺ showed the Companions how to perform wuḍūʾ and pray. He would say, "Pray like you see me praying."[29] He ﷺ showed the Companions how to perform the rites of ḥajj and said, "Learn the rituals of ḥajj from me."[30]

3. WRITING

Another way of teaching ḥadīth during the time of the Prophet ﷺ was through writing them down. Recording ḥadīth was a normal practice from the time of migration until the Prophet ﷺ left this world. Writing ḥadīth was also a practice before migration, but it was not as common. There were a number of Companions involved in writing down the aḥadīth of the Prophet ﷺ. Sometimes the Prophet ﷺ would dictate what to write to them. There were some who recorded three or four narrations, others who had recorded hundreds, and yet others who had recorded even thousands.

There is a very common misconception that the aḥadīth of the Prophet ﷺ were not documented until approximately 100 to 200 years after he ﷺ left this world. The common claim is that aḥadīth were transmitted orally for about 100 years after the death of the Prophet ﷺ, until the time of the Caliph ʿUmar ibn ʿAbd al-ʿAzīz. He then appointed Abū Bakr ibn Muḥammad ibn ʿAmr ibn Ḥazm al-Zuhrī, and others to collect ḥadīth and record them. This is the claim of a number of orientalists and western academics. Unfortunately, this claim has also crept into some circles within the Muslim community who then use it to outright reject the Sunnah or its authority, status, and value. This claim is absolutely false and is based on a lack of knowledge and ignorance of the early literary history of aḥadīth, their preservation, and their compilation.

MISUNDERSTANDING REGARDING THE WRITING OF HADITH

One of the reasons why orientalists, western academics, and some uninformed Muslims claim that the aḥadīth were not recorded during the life of the Prophet ﷺ is because of a particular narration from Abū Saʿīd al-Khudrī ﵁. Abū Saʿīd al-Khudrī ﵁ narrated that the Prophet ﷺ said, "Do not write anything from me except the Quran, and whoever has written

29 al-Bukhārī, *k. al-adab, b. rahmah al-nās wa al-bahāim*, 6008

30 Muslim, *k. al-hajj, b. istihbab ramy jamrah al-ʿaqabah yawm al-nahr rākiban*, 1297

anything from me other than the Quran should erase it."[31] This ḥadīth seems to explicitly prohibit the recording of ḥadīth.

However, research, investigation, and consideration of all other relevant narrations prove that this was not an absolute prohibition. This was a prohibition mentioned by the Prophet ﷺ during the early days of Islam so that the wording of the Quran would not become mixed with the words of the Prophet ﷺ. In the early days of Islam, those Companions who would write the Quran would also write the explanations and sayings of the Prophet ﷺ on the same material, either on the margins or between the lines. Since the Quran was being revealed and the Companions were not fully aware of the unique style of the Quran, there was a worry that the two would be mixed up. In order to prevent this confusion, the Prophet ﷺ prohibited the Companions from writing aḥadīth on the same material as the Quran. There was never an absolute prohibition for writing down ḥadīth. As a matter of fact, there is clear evidence that proves the Prophet ﷺ not only allowed for his ḥadīth to be written, but also encouraged it.

EXAMPLES OF WRITING AHADITH DURING THE LIFE OF THE PROPHET ﷺ

There are several narrations that prove that the Prophet ﷺ had given permission for his aḥadīth to be written down. The following are a few examples:

- It is narrated that once the Prophet ﷺ said, "Capture (preserve) knowledge." ʿAbdullāh ؓ asked, "How do you capture it?" The Prophet ﷺ said, "By writing."[32]
- ʿAbdullāh ibn ʿAmr ibn al-ʿĀs ؓ asked, "May I write all that I hear?" The Prophet ﷺ said, "Yes." "When you are calm and when you are angry?" The Prophet ﷺ pointed to his mouth and said, "Write, for by The One in whose Hand is my soul nothing comes out from it except the truth."[33]

---

31 Muslim, *k. al-zuhd wa al-raqāʾiq*, *b. al-tathabbut fī al-ḥadīth wa hukm kitābah al-ʿilm*

32 al-Bayhaqī, *al-madkhal ila al-sunan al-kubrā*, 238

33 Abū Dāwūd, *k. al-ʿilm*, *b. fī kitābah al-ʿilm*, 3646

- Abū Hurayrah ﷺ narrated, "There was a man among the Anṣār[34] who would sit with the Messenger of Allah ﷺ and listen to the aḥadīth of the Prophet ﷺ, and he was amazed by them but he could not remember them. So he complained about that to the Messenger of Allah ﷺ. He said: 'O Messenger of Allah! I listen to your aḥadīth and I am amazed but I cannot remember them.' So the Messenger of Allah ﷺ said: 'Help yourself with your right hand' and he motioned with his hand as if writing."[35]

In addition to that, there are several examples and instances during the life of the Prophet ﷺ of aḥadīth being written down and recorded. There were a number of Companions who had their own private and personal ḥadīth collections. The personal collection of a Companion was called a ṣaḥīfah, or booklet. As paper was scarce these small booklets were made of papyrus, parchment, palm fronds, or any other material on which it was convenient to write. They can be thought of as the personal notes of individual Companions. The following are a few examples:

- One of the best-known collections of ḥadīth that was written during the time of the Prophet ﷺ was *al-Ṣaḥīfah al-Ṣādiqah* (the Truthful Collection) by ʿAbdullāh ibn ʿAmr ibn al-ʿĀṣ ﷺ. As mentioned above, he was one of the Companions that would record the sayings of the Prophet ﷺ. It is narrated that he would write down everything he heard the Prophet ﷺ say. Some Companions even objected to how much he would write and told him that he should not write everything he heard from the Prophet ﷺ. Abū Hurayrah ﷺ said, "None of the Companions of the Prophet ﷺ has taken more ḥadīth from him than me except for ʿAbdullāh ibn ʿAmr. He used to write and I did not."[36]

  ʿAbdullāh ﷺ himself named this collection *al-Ṣaḥīfah al-Ṣādiqah*. Mujāhid ﷺ narrates: "I saw a ṣaḥīfah with ʿAbdullāh ibn ʿAmr ibn al-ʿĀṣ ﷺ so I asked him about it. He said, 'This is truthful. In it is what I heard directly from the Prophet ﷺ with no one

---

34 The Companions that were native to the city of Madinah

35 al-Tirmidhī, *kitāb al-ʿilm ʿan rasūl Allah* ﷺ, *b. mā jāʾa fī rukhsati fīhi*, 2666

36 al-Tirmidhī, *kitāb al-ʿilm ʿan rasūl Allah* ﷺ, *b. mā jāʾa fī rukhsati fīhi*, 3841

between me and him.'" His personal collection contained more than 1,000 aḥadīth and its contents have been quoted almost entirely in the *Musnad* of Imām Aḥmad ibn Ḥanbal رحمه الله. This ṣaḥīfah is described as the most reliable historical document to prove the writing of ḥadīth during the Prophet's lifetime. It was passed on in his family from generation to generation. His great-grandson, the famous muḥaddith[37] ʿAmr ibn Shuʿayb used to teach aḥadīth from it.

- ʿAlī رضي الله عنه also had his own personal collection, or ṣaḥīfah, of aḥadīth that he had written down from the Prophet ﷺ. Abū Juḥayfah said, "I asked ʿAlī رضي الله عنه, 'Do you have anything written down from the Prophet ﷺ?' He said, 'We did not write anything down from the Prophet ﷺ except for the Quran and what is in this ṣaḥīfah.'"
- Anas ibn Mālik رضي الله عنه also wrote down ḥadīth in a ṣaḥīfah that he used to carry around and show to his students. One of his students mentioned that when we used to insist that he teach us some aḥadīth, he would take out some notebooks and say, "This is what I have heard from the Messenger of Allah ﷺ, so I wrote it down and read it to him."
- There is also the ṣaḥīfah of ʿAmr ibn Ḥazm رضي الله عنه. When the Prophet ﷺ sent him as a zakāh collector to Najrān, he gave him a document consisting of the rulings of prayer, zakāh, ḥajj, ʿumrah, jihād, spoils of war, and several other subjects. Most of these narrations were incorporated into later works such as the *Muwaṭṭa*ʾ of Imām Mālik and the *Musnad* of Imām Aḥmad.
- There is also the ṣaḥīfah of Saʿd ibn ʿUbādah رضي الله عنه. He used to document the sayings and Sunnah of the Prophet ﷺ and his son used to narrate ḥadīth from it.

The above is just a small sample of written records from the time of the Prophet ﷺ that prove that aḥadīth were written during his lifetime. In *Studies in Early Ḥadīth Literature*, from which the above is taken, Dr. Azami lists fifty Companions from whom there are records of their own personal writings or students writing from them.

---

37 A scholar of ḥadīth

THE ERA OF THE COMPANIONS ﷺ

The written preservation of ḥadīth carried on during the time of the Companions ﷺ and became more widespread and popular. After the Prophet ﷺ left this world the Companions ﷺ took on the responsibility of teaching people their religion. During their time, Islam spread far and wide and centers of learning were established all across the Muslim world. Companions were sent, officially and unofficially, to different towns and cities to teach people the Quran and Sunnah. Each of these Companions would have their own informal gatherings in local mosques where they would narrate what they heard and saw from the Prophet ﷺ. Oftentimes the Companions would have what they had memorized from the Prophet ﷺ written down and would pass it on to their students. The following are just a few examples:

- Abū Hurayrah ﷺ narrated the most aḥādīth from the Prophet ﷺ. He has narrated approximately 5,374 aḥādīth. During this era either he himself wrote or had someone else write down all that he had memorized. He is reported to have several books of ḥadīth in his possession.

  For example, one of his students, Ḥasan ibn ʿAmr, read a ḥadīth to him and said I heard this ḥadīth from you. Abū Hurayrah ﷺ told him that if you have heard it from me then I have it written down. So Abū Hurayrah ﷺ took him by the hand to his house and showed him a number of books of ḥadīth that were in his possession and they found that particular ḥadīth.

  There are at least nine of his students who wrote aḥadīth from him compiling their own personal ḥadīth books. The most famous of these is the ṣaḥīfah collection of Hammām ibn Munabbih (d. 101). He was a student of Abū Hurayrah ﷺ and used to write down aḥadīth from him. This collection is known as *al-Ṣaḥīfah al-Ṣaḥīḥah* and two manuscripts of it have been found in Berlin and Damascus and were found to be almost identical. This is probably the oldest book of ḥadīth that is available today. This collection consists of 138 aḥadīth. Imām Aḥmad ﷺ collected most of it in his *Musnad* and some of the aḥadīth from it have also been narrated in al-Bukhārī and Muslim.

- Ibn 'Umar ؓ narrated 2,630 aḥadīth, the second most after Abū Hurayrah ؓ. There are authentic reports that he had a written collection of ḥadīth and at least eight of his students wrote aḥadīth from him.
- Anas ibn Mālik ؓ narrated 2,286 aḥadīth. At least sixteen people collected aḥadīth from him in written form.
- Umm al-Mu'minīn, the mother of the believers, 'Ā'ishah ؓ narrated 2,210 aḥadīth. There were at least three individuals who wrote aḥadīth from her including her nephew 'Urwah ؓ and 'Amrah bint 'Abd al-Raḥmān.
- 1,660 aḥadīth have reached us from ibn 'Abbās ؓ. There were at least nine of his students who recorded ḥadīth from him. He used to tell his students, "Capture knowledge by writing (قيدوا العلم بالكتابة)." It has been narrated that at the time of his death he had so many booklets of aḥadīth that they could be loaded on a camel.

The list of Companions who had written compilations of aḥadīth and used to dictate them to their students can go on and on. Dr. Azami writes, "In the light of the above mentioned facts, it is quite safe to assume that probably most of the aḥadīth of the Prophet ﷺ, if not all, came to be written during the life of the Companions ؓ." This era lasted from after the Prophet ﷺ left this world until the early to mid-first century.

THE ERA OF THE SUCCESSORS ؓ
(LATE 1ST CENTURY – EARLY 2ND CENTURY)

Starting from the time of 'Umar ؓ and on the Muslim world had grown quite large and the Companions of the Prophet ﷺ had travelled to a number of distant places as teachers of the Quran and Sunnah. As the Companions ؓ were slowly leaving this world a concern grew that the aḥadīth of the Prophet ﷺ should be gathered and compiled from all across the Muslim world. In response to this concern the recording and collecting of ḥadīth was officially sanctioned by the Caliph 'Umar ibn 'Abd al-'Azīz ؓ who passed away in the year 101. He sent a directive to the governor of Madīnah, Abū Bakr ibn Muḥammad ibn 'Amr ibn Ḥazm ؓ (d. 117), "Look for the knowledge of ḥadīth and get it written, as I am afraid that religious knowledge will vanish and the religious learned men will pass away (die). Do not accept anything except the aḥādīth of the Prophet ﷺ. Circulate knowledge and teach the ignorant, for knowledge does not vanish except when it is kept secretly (to oneself)." A similar directive was sent to governors across the Muslim world where it was known that the Companions of the Prophet ﷺ had settled down. These collections were sent to Damascus, where the head of the Caliphate (Khilāfah) was located. Copies were then made and spread throughout the Muslim world.

One of the main figures who played a large role in this was the great scholar Muḥammad ibn Muslim ibn Shihāb al-Zuhrī رحمه الله (d. 124) from the city of Madīnah. He was one of the teachers of Imām Mālik رحمه الله. He responded to this call with great enthusiasm and attempted the first major collection of ḥadīth. He prepared a collection of ḥadīth that came to be known as his dafātir (registers). His method of writing was subject-oriented and consisted of a separate book on each subject such as, prayer, fasting, and zakāh. In these collections he also gathered the sayings of Companions and Successors.

This literally marked the beginning of the extensive ḥadīth collections that were later compiled in the 2nd and 3rd centuries. Near the end of the first century a number of ḥadīth collections were prepared and in circulation. The following are a few examples:

- The collections of Abū Bakr ibn Muḥammad ibn ʿAmr ibn Ḥazm رحمه الله (d. 117).
- *The Risālah* (Booklet) of Sālim ibn ʿAbdullah regarding ṣadaqah.
- *The Dafātir* (Registers) of Imām Muḥammad ibn Muslim ibn Shihāb Al-Zuhrī رحمه الله (d. 124).
- *Kitāb al-Sunan* of Makḥūl رحمه الله.

COMPILATION AND PRESERVATION IN THE LATE 2ND CENTURY

The effort of gathering and compiling narrations from the Prophet ﷺ continued throughout the 2nd century with great enthusiasm and fervor. The early years of the 2nd century produced ḥadīth works that were similar to that of al-Zuhrī's in style and structure. The later part of the century witnessed writings in ḥadīth that were different in style and format. For example, the newer collections were now compiled in single volumes divided by subject matter. However, the ḥadīth scholars continued to include the sayings and fatāwā (legal verdicts) of the Companions and the Successors. This can be seen in the *Muwaṭṭa'* of Imām Mālik and the *Musnad* of Imām al-Shāfiʿī. This was also the era of the development and codification of fiqh. It was during this time that three of the four major schools of law were born.

The following are a few examples of works that were produced during the late 2nd century.

- *Kitāb al-Āthār* of Imām Abū Ḥanīfah ﵀ (d. 148) - This is the only work of ḥadīth compiled by Imām Abū Ḥanīfah ﵀ himself. Known as the "Greatest Imām," he was the leading jurist of Kūfah to whom the Ḥanafī school of thought is attributed.
- The *Muwaṭṭa'* of Imām Mālik ﵀ (d. 179) - Imām Mālik ﵀ was a master of both ḥadīth and fiqh. This is the most well-known early collection of ḥadīth whose contents are organized according to the chapters of fiqh. It contains aḥadīth of the Prophet ﷺ, legal opinions of the Companions ﵃, the Successors and some later authorities as well.
- The *Musnad* of Imām al-Shāfiʿī (﵀, d. 204) - He was the student of Imām Mālik ﵀ as well as Muḥammad ibn al-Ḥasan al-Shaybānī ﵀, the famous student of Imām Abū Ḥanīfah ﵀.
- The *Sunan* of Ibn Jurayj ﵀ (d. 150) - He is considered to be from amongst the students of the Successors (*Tabʿ al-Tabiʿīn*). He was the student of ʿAṭā' ibn Abī Rabāḥ ﵀ (d. 115), who was the student of ibn ʿAbbās and ʿAbdullāh ibn ʿUmar ﵃.
- *Muṣannaf* of Wakīʿ ibn al-Jarrāḥ ﵀ (d. 196) - He was one of the students of Imām Abū Ḥanīfah ﵀ and one of the well-known teachers of Imām al-Shāfiʿī ﵀.
- The *Jāmiʿ* of Maʿmar ibn Rāshid ﵀ (d. 154) - He was a student of Ḥammām ibn Munabbih (d. 101) and the teacher of ʿAbd al-Razzāq, the compiler of the famous *Muṣannaf*.
- The *Muṣannaf* of Ḥammād ibn Salamah ﵀ (d. 167) in Basrah - He was also from amongst the students of the Successors (*Tabiʿ al-Tabiʿīn*).
- The *Jāmiʿ* of Sufyān al-Thawrī ﵀ (d. 160) from Kufah.

- The *Jāmiʿ* of Sufyān ibn ʿUyaynah ﷺ (d. 198)
- *Kitāb al-Āthār* of Imām Muḥammad ibn Ḥasan al-Shaybānī ﷺ (d. 189)

PRESERVATION AND COMPILATION IN THE 3RD CENTURY

This era marked a new phase in the development and documentation of ḥadīth. One of the most distinctive features of this period was to separate the aḥadīth of the Prophet ﷺ from the sayings of the Companions and Successors. The ḥadīth compilers of this era on the whole observed the principles of Uṣūl al-Ḥadīth that had already gained recognition and the methodological guidelines that were developed. This was the era in which Ḥadīth Studies flourished and books on different disciplines were written.

It was in the second half of this century that the six most famous and well-recognized books of ḥadīth were compiled: *Ṣaḥīḥ al-Bukhārī*, *Ṣaḥīḥ Muslim*, *Jāmiʿ al-Tirmidhī*, *Sunan Abī Dāwūd*, *Sunan ibn Mājah*, and *Sunan al-Nasāʾī*. These books make up the six canonical books of ḥadīth known as al-Ṣiḥaḥ al-Sittah (The Six Authentic Books) or al-Kutub al-Sittah (The Six Books). Other famous works that were produced in this century include:

- *Muṣannaf* of ʿAbd al-Razzāq ﷺ (d. 211) - This is a collection of ḥadīth organized according to the chapters of fiqh. It is a very well-known ḥadīth collection and it has been published as well.
- *Muṣannaf* of Abū Bakr ibn Abī Shaybah ﷺ (d. 235) – He was one of the teachers of both Imām al-Bukhārī and Imām Muslim. This collection is also organized according to the chapters of fiqh and has been published.
- *Musnad* of Imām Aḥmad ibn Ḥanbal ﷺ (d. 241) - Contains about 40,000 narrations from 700 Companions ﷺ. It is organized based on the companion that narrated the hadīth.

Through the tireless effort of the luminaries of the first three centuries of Islam, the Sunnah of the Prophet ﷺ was gathered, analyzed, organized, codified, and preserved for future generations. Many of these works have been passed on from generation to generation and are still read, studied, explained, and commented on in seminaries and universities throughout the world.

4

HADITH LITERATURE

Each generation had its own unique circumstances, interests, and culture that influenced the scholars of ḥadīth and how they would organize their works. Every successive generation produced works building off the efforts of the previous generation that were more refined and organized. Ḥadīth scholars would organize the narrations they compiled in several different ways. As a result of these efforts and refinements a number of different genres of ḥadīth literature were produced. This chapter will examine the most common genres of ḥadīth literature.

AL-SAHIFAH

Al-Ṣaḥīfah, translated as a booklet, is a term used to refer to very early rudimentary collections of ḥadīth. These collections marked the earliest stage in the documentation of ḥadīth. A number of Companions ﷺ had their own personal ṣaḥīfah. For example, as mentioned earlier ʿAbdullāh ibn ʿAmr ibn Al-ʿĀṣ ﷺ had a collection he called *al-Ṣaḥīfah al-Ṣādiqah* and the *Ṣaḥīfah* of ʿAlī ﷺ.

These small booklets would have consisted of papyrus, parchment (tanned animal skins), or palm fronds. Usually, these were not public documents; they were the private notes of individual Companions ﷺ. In these personal collections aḥadīth were simply recorded without any order or classification. These collections started during the lifetime of the Prophet ﷺ and continued until the early second century.

AL-MUSANNAF

Al-Muṣannaf is the title used to describe a ḥadīth collection that has been organized by topic. These collections are considered to be the first organized works of Islamic Scholarship. The Muṣannaf did not focus exclusively on the aḥadīth of the Prophet ﷺ. Rather they are collections of aḥadīth, sayings and rulings of Companions as well us some successors organized by subject matter. In these collections aḥadīth belonging to particular themes were classified under separate titles and chapters. They were arranged into chapters dealing with different legal or ritual questions. They can be thought of as early works on Islamic Law that represent the diversity of sources from which legal and doctrinal answers could be sought during the first two centuries of Islam. They served as an important resource for later ḥadīth literature. This genre of ḥadīth literature started around the middle of the 2nd century. The most famous collections in this genre are the *Muwaṭṭa'* of Imām Mālik ؓ (d. 179), the *Muṣannaf* of ʿAbd al-Razzāq ؓ (d. 211) and the *Muṣannaf* of Ibn Abī Shaybah ؓ (d. 235). All three of these have been published and are available today.

AL-MUSNAD

A musnad is a collection organized according to isnād, or the chain of narrators. For example, all the aḥadīth narrated from a certain Companion would fall into one chapter, and then all those narrated from another in the next and so on. So all the aḥadīth that were narrated by one Companion, regardless of subject matter, were put under his or her name.

The musnad compilers differed in their arrangement of names of Companions. Some of them begin with the four rightly guided Caliphs, followed by the remaining six who had been given the glad tidings of Paradise. Some are organized alphabetically.

In these collections greater attention was paid to the chain of narrators. The main purpose of a musnad was to compile the largest amount of ḥadīth for the sake of preservation and record. That is why they are considered to be encyclopedic and reference works. This genre of ḥadīth literature started during the latter half of the 2nd century. The most well-known is the *Musnad* of Imām Aḥmad ibn Ḥanbal (ﷺ, d. 241).

AL-JAMI'

Jāmiʿ is the title given to a ḥadīth collection that includes all of the major topics or subjects addressed in the aḥadīth of the Prophet ﷺ. There are eight primary topics or subjects covered in the aḥadīth of the Prophet ﷺ:

1. ʿAqā'id (Beliefs/Creed)
2. Aḥkām (Legal Rulings)
3. Siyar (History and Biography of the Prophet)
4. Ādāb (Social Etiquette)
5. Tafsīr (Quranic Exegesis)
6. Ashrāṭ (Signs of the Day of Judgment)
7. Fitan (Trials and Tribulations)
8. Manāqib (Virtues of the Companions).

A typical Jāmiʿ would include chapters on each of these subjects.

This genre of ḥadīth literature is considered to be the most comprehensive approach in terms of collection because of the broad range of topics it covers. It started during the third century. The collections of Imām al-Bukhārī, Imām Muslim, and Imām al-Tirmidhī ﷺ are considered to be amongst the jawāmiʿ because they contain aḥadīth on all eight of these subjects.

Within this genre and time period there was a new focus on producing collections of aḥadīth with an emphasis on authenticity. They focused on including those aḥadīth that they considered or deemed to be authentic. The first to produce ḥadīth collections devoted only to narrations whose asānīd (chains) they felt met the requirements of authenticity were Imām Muḥammad ibn Ismāʿīl al-Bukhārī (d. 256) and Imām Muslim ibn al-Ḥajjāj al-Naysābūrī (d. 261). Their works are known as the ṣaḥīḥayn, or the two authentic collections and are without a doubt the two most famous ḥadīth collections in existence.

It is important to note that the term ṣaḥīḥayn is not used in the exclusive sense; there are ṣaḥīḥ aḥādīth in all the other major collections. Also, it was not their intention to compile every single ṣaḥīḥ ḥadīth in existence nor did they make that a condition upon themselves.

SUNAN

A sunan is a ḥadīth collection that is organized according to the well-known chapters of fiqh or Islamic Jurisprudence. For example, ṭahārah (purification), ṣalāh (prayer), zakāh (obligatory charity), ṣawm (fasting), ḥajj (pilgrimage), nikāḥ (marriage), ṭalāq (divorce) and buyūʿ (transactions). The Book of Ṭahārah will then have separate chapters for wuḍūʾ (ablution), tayammum (dry ablution) and ghusl (purificatory bath).

Works that fall under this category consist of those aḥādīth that are used to derive legal rulings, which are known as aḥādīth al-aḥkām (أحاديث الأحكام). This genre of ḥadīth literature also became popular in the 3rd century. The most famous sunan collections are:

- The *Sunan* of Abū Dāwūd
- The *Sunan* of al-Nasāʾī
- The *Sunan* of Ibn Mājah

All three of these are considered to be part of the "Six Books" or the six canonical collections of ḥadīth.

AL-MUJAM

A muʿjam is a ḥadīth collection in which the contents appear in alphabetical order under the names of the narrators and their teachers or the cities and tribes to which the narrators belong. The collection can be organized alphabetically according to the names of the companions, teachers, or certain narrators. An example of this is *al-Muʿjam al-Kabīr* by Abū al-Qāsim Sulaymān ibn Aḥmad al-Ṭabarānī. This genre of ḥadīth literature appeared after the sunans in the late 3rd century.

AL-MUSTADRAK

A mustadrak is a ḥadīth collection in which the compiler has supplemented the work of a previous compiler or compilers. Having accepted the conditions laid down by previous compilers, the later scholar collects other aḥādīth that they find to fulfill those conditions but have been left out of the previous works. For example, the *Mustadrak ʿala al-Ṣaḥīḥayn* of al-Ḥākim al-Naysābūrī (d. 405). He tried to collect narrations that met the conditions of Imām al-Bukhārī and Muslim but were not included in their works.

AL-MUSTAKHRAJ

A mustakhraj is a ḥadīth collection in which the compiler gathers the narrations from another book with his own asānīd, or chain of narrators. The narrations are essentially the same, but the chain of narrators is different. A ḥadīth scholar would take an existing collection and use it as a template for his own book; for every ḥadīth found in the template collection the author of the mustakhraj would provide his own narration of that ḥadīth. For example, there is a mustakhraj on *Ṣaḥīḥ al-Bukhārī* and *Ṣaḥīḥ Muslim*. This genre came about in the 4th century.

AL-JUZ'

A juz' is a ḥadīth collection that focuses on the narrations of one single narrator, a companion or someone else, or a collection that focuses on aḥādīth regarding one single theme or subject. For example, a collection that focuses only on the narrations of Abū Bakr ؓ would be called *Juz' Abī Bakr*. Another example is the *Juz' fī Qiyām al-Layl* by al-Marwazī. In this collection, he gathered those narrations that talk about qiyām al-layl, the night prayer.

AL-SHARH

One of the most important genres of ḥadīth literature that appeared later on is a sharḥ, commentary. These commentaries were usually written on the more well-known and widely-used ḥadīth collections.

A sharḥ serves two general purposes. First, they assist students in the basic task of reading and understanding difficult phrases, names, and obscure meanings embedded in the chains or texts of the narrations. Second, they provided scholars an opportunity to elaborate in detail on any legal, dogmatic, ritual, or historical issue they found relevant to the aḥadīth in the books they were discussing. The vast majority of commentaries were devoted to the books in the ḥadīth canon. The most famous of these works are Ibn Ḥajar al-ʿAsqalānī's ﷺ (d. 852) *Fatḥ al-Bārī* and Imām al-Nawawi''s commentary on *Ṣaḥīḥ Muslim*.

Ḥadīth commentaries continue to be written to this very day. For example, the most famous commentary of *Jāmiʿ al-Tirmidhī* is *Tuḥfah al-Aḥwadhī* (Gem of the Competent) written by the Indian Scholar ʿAbd al-Raḥmān al-Mubārakfūrī ﷺ (1935). Similarly, the largest commentary on the *Muwaṭṭa* of Imām Mālik is written by the Indian Scholar Muḥammad Zakariyya Kāndahlawī ﷺ (1982) entitled *Awjaz al-Masālik ila Muwaṭṭa' Mālik*. Recently Muftī Taqi Usmani completed a commentary on *Ṣaḥīḥ Muslim* entitled *Takmilah Fatḥ al-Mulhim*, which is a completion of his teacher's commentary on *Ṣaḥīḥ Muslim* entitled *Fatḥ al-Mulhim*.

5

WELL-KNOWN HADITH WORKS & THEIR COMPILERS

By the end of the 4th century there were a number of well-known and accepted ḥadīth collections in circulation throughout the Muslim world. By the middle of the fourth century a selection of these books were accepted amongst scholars and students of ḥadīth as being authoritative and representative of the vast corpus of ḥadīth. Initially they included *Ṣaḥīḥ al-Bukhārī*, *Ṣaḥīḥ Muslim*, *Sunan Abī Dāwūd*, and *Sunan al-Nasā'ī*. After some time the collection of Imām al-Tirmidhī was included within this list along with the work of ibn Mājah. These six books came to be known as al-Kutub al-Sittah or al-Ṣiḥāḥ al-Sittah. They are considered to be the six canonical books of ḥadīth. This chapter will give a brief introduction to these famous works and a few others along with a short biography of their authors.

MUWATTA' OF IMAM MALIK رحمه الله

The *Muwaṭṭa'* of Imām Mālik is the most famous muṣannaf that is taught and studied throughout the world today. The word muwaṭṭa' literally means "the travelled path". His full name is Mālik ibn Anas ibn Mālik ibn Abī ʿĀmir. He was born in Madīnah in the year 92 and passed away in Madinah in the year 179. He is one of the greatest scholars of ḥadīth and fiqh the world has ever seen and the founder of one of the four main schools of thought. It was said regarding him, "No fatwā is to be given while Mālik is in Madinah."

As mentioned earlier the *Muwaṭṭa'* itself is a mixture of Prophetic ḥadīth, the rulings of his Companions ﷺ, the practice of the scholars of Madīnah, and his own personal opinions. It contains 1,720 reports: 527 ḥadīth, 613 statements from the Companions ﷺ, and 285 statements from the successors and the remaining are his own. It was considered to be the most authentic book after the Quran, before the compilation of *Ṣaḥīḥ al-Bukhārī*. He initially started compiling this work at the request of the Abbasid Caliph Abū Ja'far al-Manṣūr. He wanted Imām Mālik ﷺ to compose a comprehensive book of law based on the Prophet's ﷺ Sunnah, which could then be implemented throughout the Islamic world. But once it was completed Imām Mālik ﷺ declined to have it endorsed as the official book on Islamic Law.[38]

Once Hārūn al-Rashīd told Imām Mālik that he wanted to make copies of his *Muwaṭṭa'*, distribute them across the Muslim world and make people follow it. Imām Mālik said, "O Leader of the Faithful. Indeed the differences of the scholars are a mercy from Allah on this nation. Everyone follows what is correct according to them; they are all upon guidance and they are all sincere to Allah." There are a number of exhaustive commentaries that were written on this work later on. For example, *al-Tamhīd* by ibn 'Abd al-Barr and *Awjaz al-Masālik ila Muwaṭṭa' Mālik* by al-Kāndahlawī.

SAHIH AL-BUKHARI

Imām al-Bukhārī entitled his magnum opus *al-Jāmi' al-Ṣaḥīḥ al-Musnad al-Mukhtaṣar min Ḥadīth Rasūl Allah wa Sunanihī wa Ayyāmihī*. His full name is Abū 'Abdillah Muḥammad ibn Ismā'īl ibn Ibrāhīm ibn al-Mughīrah al-Bukhārī ﷺ. He was born in Bukhārah in the year 194 and passed away in the year 256.

Imām al-Bukhārī ﷺ began his studies under the guidance of his mother in his native city. After finishing his initial studies, at the age of 11, he immersed himself in the study of ḥadīth. Within six years he had mastered the knowledge of all the ḥadīth scholars of Bukharah as well as everything in the books that were available to him. Not only did he memorize all the aḥadīth but he also memorized the narrators and their biographies: the location and dates of their birth, death, and so on.

38 Ibn 'Abd al-Barr, *al-Istidhkār*

At the age of 16 he started travelling. He travelled to Makkah with his mother and brother to perform ḥajj and from there he started a series of journeys as a student of knowledge. He travelled to all of the major centers of Islamic Learning. He stayed in Basrah for four to five years and in the Hejaz[39] for six. He travelled to Egypt, Nishapur, Marw, and Baghdad. His travels continued for nearly four decades. Within that time Imām al-Bukhārī had gathered aḥadīth from over a thousand teachers.

Imām al-Bukhārī was blessed with an amazing memory. Once when he arrived in Baghdad the scholars gathered there to test his famous memory. They appointed 10 men and every one of them narrated 10 aḥadīth. All of them intentionally changed the isnād (chain) and put it with a different matn (text). One by one they read the distorted aḥadīth to him and asked whether he knew it or not. To all 100 hundred he replied, "Not known to me." After the questions were done he systematically went through and corrected all 100 narrations! He was known for his God-consciousness, good character, and generosity.

Imām al-Bukhārī ؒ devoted 16 years to the compilation of this unparalleled work. He was inspired to undertake this compilation after one of his teachers, Isḥāq ibn Rāhawayh ؒ, commented in passing, "if you were to compile a short but comprehensive collection (kitāban mukhtaṣaran) of the authentic Sunnah of the Messenger of Allah ﷺ." After this the idea stuck in his mind until he saw a dream in which he was standing in front of the Prophet ﷺ with a fan in his hand. He understood it to mean that he was blessed with the task of removing doubts and impurity from the Sunnah of the Prophet ﷺ.

He sifted through 600,000 aḥādīth selecting 9,082 for his *Ṣaḥīḥ*. If repetitions are excluded, the actual number of aḥādīth is 2,062. He used to offer two units of prayer every time he decided to include a ḥadīth in his collection. He wrote a good portion of the book in Makkah and Madinah and the rest in Basrah, Kufah, and Bukharah. When he completed his work, he showed it to some of the leading scholars of his time such as Imām Aḥmad ibn Ḥanbal ؒ, Yaḥya ibn Maʿīn ؒ, and ʿAli ibn al-Madīnī who all approved of it.

The book itself is divided into 96 books and a total of 3,450 chapters. Each chapter is given a title that is descriptive of its contents. One of the

39 A sub-portion of the Arabian Peninsula

most unique features of this work is the chapter headings. Imām al-Bukhārī was not only an expert in ḥadīth but he was also an expert in fiqh. He was a mujtahid[40] and the chapter titles indicate the legal implication or ruling the reader should derive from the subsequent aḥādīth. As the saying goes, "The fiqh of Imām al-Bukhārī ﵀ is in his headings." The titles also include a short comment from him or a report from a Companion or Successor clarifying the aḥādīth. The finished work is not simply a ḥadīth collection; it is a massive expression of Imām al-Bukhārī's understanding of Islamic Law and Belief.

SAHIH MUSLIM

The second of the two most famous ṣaḥīḥ collections is that of Imām Muslim ibn al-Ḥajjāj al-Naysābūrī ﵀. He was born in the year 206 and passed away in the year 261. Similar to Imām al-Bukhārī, he learned the Islamic Sciences at a very young age and then focused his attention on the study of the aḥādīth of the Prophet ﷺ.

He travelled widely visiting the main centers of ḥadīth study in Persia, Iraq, Syria, Egypt, and the Ḥijāz. He attended the gatherings of the most learned ḥadīth scholars of his time including Isḥāq ibn Rāhawayh (one of the teachers of Imām al-Bukhārī), Aḥmad ibn Ḥanbal ﵀, and Imām al-Bukhārī. He had learned aḥādīth from hundreds of teachers. He settled down in Naysābūr and earned a living from a small business. He devoted his life to the service of the Sunnah.

The original title of his work is *al-Musnad al-Ṣaḥīḥ al-Mukhtaṣar min al-Sunan bi Naql al-ʿAdl ʿan al-ʿAdl ʿan Rasūlillāh*. For this work Imām Muslim ﵀ sifted through over 300,000 aḥādīth and selected 7,479, or 3,033 if repetitions are excluded, over a period of fifteen years. Imām Muslim also organized the aḥādīth by subject matter and compiled all the aḥādīth on the same subject with their various chains under one chapter. His system and method of organization was more refined than Imām al-Bukhārī's.

One of the reasons that inspired Imām Muslim to compile this work was that the works of ḥadīth that were available were difficult to use and to defend the Sunnah of the Prophet ﷺ. Dr. Brown writes, "Muslim wrote his *Ṣaḥīḥ* as a response to what he saw as the laxity and misplaced priorities of ḥadīth scholars and transmitters. He believed that those scholars who strove

40 A legal scholar capable of deriving laws from their original sources

to collect as many ḥadīth as possible regardless of their quality were doing so to only to impress others. Muslim expressed serious concern over would-be ḥadīth scholars who transmitted material of dubious nature to the exclusion of well-known and well-authenticated ḥadīth. They provided this material to the common people when in fact it is the ḥadīth scholars' duty to leave the common folk with trustworthy reports only..."[41] It took him 15 years to compile this work.

JAMI OF IMAM AL-TIRMIDHI

The *Jāmiʿ* of Imām al-Tirmidhī is included within the six canonical works of ḥadīth. It was compiled by Abū ʿĪsa Muḥammad ibn ʿĪsa al-Tirmidhī (209-279). He travelled extensively throughout the Muslim world to seek out narrations of the Prophet ﷺ. His travels allowed him to learn from the ḥadīth scholars of the major centers of Islam such as Iraq, Persia, and Khurasan. He was a student of Imām al-Bukhārī, Imām Muslim, and Imām Abū Dāwūd ﵏. After his extensive travels he returned to his hometown of Khurasān and compiled his *Jāmiʿ* over a period of twenty years.

Imām al-Tirmidhī, similar to his teacher Imām al-Bukhārī, was blessed with a very unique and incredible memory. There is an amazing story mentioned from his early days as a student. He had studied with a well-known ḥadīth scholar who dictated a number of aḥādīth to him that filled about 16 pages. Unfortunately, Imām al-Tirmidhī lost them before he could review them. After some time, he was given the opportunity to learn from him again. The ḥadīth scholar said that he would dictate the same aḥādīth he narrated to him last time and that Imām al-Tirmidhī should double check his notes. Out of fear of being thought of as careless Imām al-Tirmidhī picked up some blank sheets of paper and looked at them as though they had the aḥādīth written on them as the scholar dictated. Soon the teacher noticed the sheets were blank and became very angry. Imām al-Tirmidhī explained that he remembered every single word that had been dictated to him by memory. Accordingly, the muḥaddith challenged him to recite the aḥādīth from his memory. Imām al-Tirmidhī recited all of the aḥādīth without a single mistake. The muḥaddith was shocked so he narrated another 40 aḥādīth to him and asked him to repeat them. Without hesitation Imām al-Tirmidhī

41 Brown, *Hadith Muhammad's Legacy in the Medieval and Modern World*

repeated the aḥādīth verbatim!

Jāmiʿ al-Tirmidhī is considered to be one of the most important works of ḥadīth literature. A unique feature of his work is that he attempted to record those aḥādīth that were practiced and accepted by the jurists and community at large, except for two specific ḥadīth. He said, "Every ḥadīth that is in this book is acted upon and some scholars have acted upon it, except for two ḥadīth. The ḥadīth, "If he drinks a fourth time then kill him" and the ḥadīth "he combined between ẓuhr and ʿaṣr in Madīnah without fear and travel".

He organized his work according to chapters (abwāb) starting off with those chapters that deal with the well-known topics of fiqh or Islamic Jurisprudence. For example, ṭahārah, ṣalah, zakāh, ṣawm, ḥajj, nikāḥ, ṭalāq, and buyūʿ. He then brings chapters that deal with all of the major topics or subjects addressed in the aḥādīth of the Prophet ﷺ, which include siyar (History and Biography of the Prophet ﷺ), ādāb (Social Etiquette), tafsīr (Quranic Exegesis), ashrāṭ (Signs of the Day of Judgment), fitan (Trials and Tribulations), and manāqib (Virtues of the Companions). That is why his work is considered to be a jāmiʿ.

Each heading is derived from the narrations that follow, saying "what has come regarding topic X". The title of the chapter either mentions the name of the issue or the ruling that he wants to highlight. Under each of these chapter headings he brings one or two narrations. Afterwards he gives his opinion about the grade of the ḥadīth; whether it is authentic, good, or weak. He graded aḥādīth as ṣaḥīḥ, ḥasan, ṣaḥīḥ ḥasan, ḥasan ṣaḥīḥ, gharīb, ḍaʿīf, and munkar. Some of these terms were unique to him and he defined them in his own way. He also mentions the opinions of earlier jurists, scholars, and imāms regarding the subject matter of the ḥadīth. He also indicates if there were aḥādīth transmitted by other Companions concerning the same subject by saying "wa fī al-bāb" (and regarding this topic).

According to one count, there are 3,956 narrations in this monumental work. It is unanimously included within the "six books" that are considered to be the ḥadīth canon. It was widely accepted during his own life-time. al-Tirmidhī said, "I compiled this book and then presented it to the scholars of Hejaz, Iraq, and Khurasan and they were all pleased with it." He also said, "Whoever has this book in their house, it is as if they have a speaking prophet in their house."

SUNAN ABU DAWUD

This is the famous collection of Imām Abū Dāwūd Sulaymān ibn al-Ashʿath al-Sijistānī ﵀. He was born in the year 202 in the well-known region of Sijistan in Khurasan and passed away in the year 275 in the city of Basrah and is buried next to the great scholar, Sufyān al-Thawrī ﵀.

Similar to the previous scholars of ḥadīth, after completing his initial studies of the Islamic Sciences he dedicated himself to the study of ḥadīth. He travelled extensively at a very young age. His pursuit of ḥadīth took him to Hejaz, Egypt, Basrah, Kufah, Baghdad, Damascus, Khurasan, Rayy, Hirat, and Tarasus. He was able to meet and study with the most knowledgeable ḥadīth scholars of his time. He was well-known for his knowledge, scholarship, God-consciousness honesty, and worship. He was also known to have a photographic memory.

His *Sunan* is considered to be the first work ever produced in this genre as well as the most comprehensive. Throughout his travels and years as a student he was able to collect over 500,000 aḥādīth. Out of this vast collection he selected 5,274 aḥādīth, 4,800 without repetition, to record in this collection. It is said that it took him approximately 20 years to compile this work while he was living in Tarasūs.

One of the most unique features of this collection is that it deals exclusively and exhaustively with those aḥādīth that are of a legal nature. It is considered to be so comprehensive on legal aḥādīth and on ḥalāl and ḥarām that "it is sufficient for the mujtahid" to obtain knowledge of the ḥalāl and the ḥarām from Abū Dāwūd. He himself writes that he knows of "nothing after the Quran more essential for people to learn than this book, and a person would suffer no loss if he did not take in any more knowledge after it."

His work includes narrations that are ṣaḥīḥ,[42] ḥasan, and some that are ḍaʿīf. However, whenever Imām Abū Dāwūd brings a weak ḥadīth he identifies it and explains why he considers it to be weak. This also implies that whenever he does not specify weakness in a ḥadīth it is considered to be sound and acceptable to him. This collection was widely circulated during his own lifetime.

42 These terms will be defined later

SUNAN AL-NASA'I

This is the celebrated work of Imām Abū ʿAbd al-Raḥmān Aḥmad ibn Shuʿayb al-Nasāʾī. He was born in the year 215 in Nasa, a town in Khurasan and passed away in the year 303 in Damascus. He received his early education in his home province and then travelled widely in pursuit of ḥadīth studies. At the age of 15 he travelled to Balkh and later travelled to Iraq, Syria, Hejaz and Egypt. He eventually settled down in Egypt. He was recognized as the leading ḥadīth scholar of his time and was known for his knowledge and precision in recording. He was also known to be very brave. He participated in jihād with the governor of Egypt. In the military camp he would guide the governor and the army, teach them the Sunnah of the Prophet ﷺ and ask them to follow it.

The collection consists of 5,000 aḥādīth of a legal nature, a large number of which had already appeared in previous collections. This particular collection was compiled in two stages. The initial worked he compiled contained aḥādīth that were ṣaḥīḥ, ḥasan, and ḍaʿīf. This larger work was entitled *al-Sunan al-Kubrā*. Imām al-Nasāʾī presented this larger work to the Abbasid governor of Ramallah in Palestine. The governor asked whether all the aḥādīth in the collection were ṣaḥīḥ or not. Imām al-Nasāʾī told him it contains both ṣaḥīḥ and ḥasan narrations and those close to them. So he asked him to compile a work that contained only ṣaḥīḥ ḥadīth. Imām al-Nasāʾī revised his work and extracted a smaller collection known as *al-Sunan al-Ṣughrā* that he entitled *al-Mujtabā min al-Sunan*. The *Mujtabā* is the collection known as *Sunan al-Nasāʾī* and it is considered to be one of the most reliable works after the Ṣaḥīḥayn. It contains very few weak aḥādīth and is one of the best collections in terms of classification and organization.

SUNAN IBN MAJAH

This is the celebrated work of Imām Abū ʿAbdillāh Muḥammad ibn Yazīd al-Rabīʿ, also known as ibn Mājah al-Qazwīnī. He was born in the year 209 in Qazwin and passed away in the year 273. He also started his pursuit of ḥadīth studies at a very early age and travelled extensively across the Muslim world to sit with the great ḥadīth masters of his time. He was known for his scholarship and good character. He was the leading ḥadīth scholar of Qazwin and was also well-known as a leading mufassir of the Quran.

In this collection he compiled 4,341 aḥādīth divided into 38 books, which are further divided into 1,500 chapters. Out of these 4,341 narrations, 3,002 have also been included in the other five main books of ḥadīth. Out of the remaining 1,339: 428 are ṣaḥīḥ, 199 are ḥasan, 613 are ḍaʿīf, and 99 are munkar. He included all types of narrations in this work, which is why his work was not included in the "Six Books" until the early 6th century. Ibn Mājah's collection has very little repetition and is one of the best in terms of arrangement of chapters and subchapters.

6

AL-ISNAD

CHAIN OF NARRATORS

As mentioned earlier, every single ḥadīth consists of two parts; the chain of narrators (sanad/isnād) and the text (matn). The isnād is perhaps the most important tool that was used to ensure and preserve the authenticity of the aḥādīth of the Prophet ﷺ. It allowed the scholars of ḥadīth to sift through the hundreds of thousands of narrations and determine which were authentic and which were weak. That is why the famous ḥadīth scholar of the second century, ʿAbdullah ibn al-Mubārak ؒ (d. 181) said, "Isnād is an intrinsic part of this religion. If it was not for the isnād then anyone could have said whatever they wanted to say."[43] The system of isnād is used to verify the authenticity of the report itself. It is used to make sure that the words or deeds of the Prophet ﷺ were passed down from teacher to student correctly and accurately. There is a whole branch of ḥadīth studies dedicated to the study of the reliability of narrators from each generation called Asmāʾ al-Rijāl. It serves as an encyclopedic reference used to determine if the narrator is upright and reliable or weak and unreliable when it comes to moral integrity, accuracy, and verifiable transmission.

43 الإسناد من الدين. فلولا الإسناد لقال من شاء ما شاء

ORIGINS OF THE ISNAD

Since the beginning of ḥadīth narration, from the time of the Prophet ﷺ, a lot of care and attention had been given to ensure that the aḥādīth of the Prophet ﷺ were being preserved and narrated accurately. Part of the reason why so much care and attention was given to accurate and precise narrations of his words is because the Prophet ﷺ warned against falsely attributing things to him.

There are several narrations in which the Prophet ﷺ warns against falsely attributing statements to him. The Prophet ﷺ said, "Whoever tells a lie about me intentionally, then let him take his seat in the fire."[44] Similarly the Prophet ﷺ said, "Ascribing false things to me is not like ascribing false things to anyone else. Whosoever tells a lie against me intentionally then surely let him occupy his seat in Hellfire."[45] In another ḥadīth the Prophet ﷺ said, "Whoever narrated a ḥadīth from me thinking it to be false then he is one of the two liars."[46] In another narration the Prophet ﷺ said, "It is justifiable for a person who says whatever they hear to be considered a liar."[47]

These and similar other warnings influenced the Companions and following generations of Muslims to exercise extreme caution in the transmission and narration of ḥadīth. Based off ample evidence on how the Companions narrated and verified reports it can be said that the rudimentary system of isnād was established during the time of the Prophet ﷺ. It was a common practice during the time of the Prophet ﷺ for the Companions to narrate aḥādīth to one another. Some of them even made special arrangements to attend the Prophet's lessons in shifts and then later inform each other of what they learnt. When informing each other they would use phrases such as, "I saw the Prophet ﷺ do such and such" or "the Prophet ﷺ said such and such".

During the era of the Companions, the borders of Islam expanded towards the East up to and into Iran and to the West into Egypt and North Africa. The Companions settled in the major centers throughout the Muslim world teaching the Quran and Sunnah of the Prophet ﷺ. They would say to

44 al-Tirmidhī, *k. al-ʾilm ʿan rasūlillah* ﷺ, *b. mā jāʾa fī taʾẓīm al-kadhib ʿalā rasūlillah*, 2659
45 al-Bukhārī, *k. al-janāʾiz, b. mā yukrahu min al-niyāḥah ʿalā al-mayit*, 1291
46 al-Tirmidhī, *k. al-ʾilm ʿan rasūlillah* ﷺ, *b. mā jāʾa fī man rawā ḥadīthan wa huwa yarā annahu kadhib*, 2662
47 Abū Dāwūd, *k. al-adab, b. fī tashdīd fī al-kadhib*, 4992

their students, the Tābiʿūn (Successors), "I saw the Prophet ﷺ do such and such" or "I heard the Prophet ﷺ say such and such". This is how the isnād was born.

The Tābiʿūn carried on the tradition of their teachers and taught their students. During their time Islam had spread into India, Afghanistan, Russia, China, and Spain. They would narrate aḥādīth saying "I heard such and such Companion say that he saw the Prophet ﷺ do such and such." With that the second link in the chain of narration was added. By the end of the 1st century the system of isnād was refined and fully developed.

THE EXPANSION OF THE ISNAD

Generally speaking the further down the chain from the Prophet ﷺ the greater the number of narrators. For example, a ḥadīth that may have been narrated by only one companion may have ten students in the next generation, and in turn these ten students may have twenty or even thirty students each belonging to different countries and provinces.

An example of this is the following narration: Naṣr ibn ʿAlī al-Jahdamī and Ḥāmid ibn ʿUmar al-Bakrāwī informed us saying: Bishr ibn al-Mufaḍḍal informed us from Khālid, from ʿAbdullah ibn Shaqīq from Abū Hurayrah that the Prophet Muhammad ﷺ said: "If anyone among you wakes up from sleep, he must not put his hand in a utensil until he has washed it three times, since he doesn't know where his hand was whilst asleep."

At least thirteen students narrated this ḥadīth from Abū Hurayrah: eight from Madinah, one from Kufah, two from Basrah, one from Yemen, and one from Syria. Sixteen students then narrated this ḥadīth from them: six from Madinah, four from Basrah, two from Kufah, one from Makkah, one from Yemen, one from Khurasan, and one from Hims. This shows how ḥadīth spread throughout the Muslim world and how the number of narrators increased in each generation.

The spread of the isnād system gave rise to two unique yet related branches of ḥadīth studies:

1. Biographies (ʿilm al-ruwāt)
2. Critique and Validation (al-jarḥ wa al-taʿdīl)

7

BIOGRAPHIES OF HADITH NARRATORS & CRITIQUE AND VALIDATION

'ILM TARIKH AL-RUWAT & AL-JARH WA AL-TADIL

The branch of Ḥadīth Studies that deals with the biographies of narrators is known as ʿIlm al-Rijāl or Asmāʾ al-Rijāl. This branch of ḥadīth studies is concerned mainly with the biographical data, chronology, life histories, academic achievements, teachers, students, school of following, political leaning, and views of ḥadīth narrators, and the statements of other people concerning them. Basically, it deals with any information that is relevant to their reliability as narrators as well as anything that helps to explain and identify the personality and character of the narrator. It is also concerned with the generation (ṭabaqah) and time frame in which the narrators lived.

One of the most important things looked at is the date and place of birth and death. Based on this information the ḥadīth masters were able to tell if the chain was connected or not. For example, the ḥadīth scholar of Syria, Ismāʿīl ibn ʿAyyāsh (d. 182), asked a man concerning a ḥadīth he had narrated from the tābiʿī Khālid ibn Maʿdān, "When did you write ḥadīth from Khālid ibn Maʿdān?" He replied, "In the year 113." Ibn ʿAyyāsh commented, "Did you hear the ḥadīth from him seven years after his death? Ibn Maʿdān passed away in the year 106!"

There are many encyclopedic works that have been written in this branch of ḥadīth studies gathering the biological information of thousands of ḥadīth narrators throughout the early generations of Islam. One of the earliest works in this field is the *Kitāb al-Ṭabaqāt al-Kabīr* in fifteen volumes of ibn Saʿd al-

Zuhrī ﷺ (d. 230). It contains the biographies of over 4,000 narrators and it covers the biographies of most of the important narrators of ḥadīth. Imām al-Bukhārī's (d. 256) *al-Tārīkh al-Kābīr* dealt with over 40,000 narrators. Unfortunately, no complete manuscript of this work exists. Only portions of it have been preserved. Ibn Ḥajar al-ʿAsqalānī (852), in his *Tahdhīb al-Tahdhīb,* recorded the biographies of over 12,000 ḥadīth narrators.

The data collected in these extensive and exhaustive works provides the basic tools for ḥadīth criticism and the application of rules pertaining to declaring narrators reliable or unreliable.

Another branch of Ḥadīth Studies closely related to ʿIlm al-Rijāl is that of al-Jarḥ wa al-Taʿdīl, referred to as Critique and Validation. This branch of Ḥadīth Studies is concerned mainly with the reliability or unreliability of ḥadīth narrators and compiles information which either proves them to be upright and reliable or weak and unreliable. Al-Taʿdīl means establishing a narrator as upright in the moral sense and reliable in terms of memory and accuracy. Al-Jarḥ literally means to wound and it refers to declaring a ḥadīth narrator as having suspect character and being unreliable.

Works in this field started appearing around the early 3rd century; however ḥadīth narrator criticism and isnād evaluation started from the era of the Companions and evolved and developed organically along with the spread and growth of ḥadīth transmission. For example, there was formal ḥadīth criticism carried out by the giants of the 2nd century such as Shuʿbah ibn al-Ḥajjāj (d. 104), Mālik ibn Anas (d. 179), Sufyān al-Thawrī (d. 161), and Sufyān ibn ʿUyaynah (d. 198).

These scholars are the individuals who began the process of collecting people's narrations and examining their work and their character to determine if they could be trusted. This work was carried on by the three giants of the late 2nd and early 3rd century; Yaḥya ibn Maʿīn (ﷺ, 233), Imām Aḥmad ibn Ḥanbal (ﷺ, 241), and ʿAlī al-Madīnī (ﷺ, 234). Their students refined ḥadīth criticism into its most exact and lasting form: the two Shaykhs, al-Bukhārī and Muslim.

Whenever the reliability of a ḥadīth narrator is questioned and there is an investigation into their character and knowledge two things can happen:

1. the available information proves that they are upright and reliable (this is known as taʿdīl or proving someone to be upright and reliable)

2. the available information shows that the narrator is unreliable and that his character is questionable (this is referred to as jarḥ or critique)

The methods applied in ḥadīth criticism were focused on the reliability of the narrator. In order to accept a ḥadīth as authentic or even good it is not enough for the text to be accurate and sound but the narrators should also be upright, credible, and accurate. To determine these factors the scholars of ḥadīth developed a set of criteria that allowed them to grade the ḥadīth narrators as reliable or unreliable.

When analyzing a narrator, the scholars of ḥadīth looked at two major factors:

1. al-ʿadālah (moral uprightness)
2. al-ḍabṭ (accuracy)

Al-ʿAdālah refers to the narrator's moral character. It is an innate quality or nature (faculty) that causes a person to be God-conscious and well-mannered. God-consciousness (taqwā) is staying away from major sins and not being persistent in minor sins. Well-mannered refers to one's behavior and etiquettes related to everyday affairs such as eating, drinking, and manner of speaking.

The ʿadālah of a narrator is determined mostly through their biographical information. It is also dependent on their reputation and acceptance amongst other ḥadīth scholars. Al-ʿadālah is used to evaluate a narrator's character, belief, and level of piety.

There are five factors that are considered to negatively affect the ʿadālah of a narrator:

1. lying (al-kidhb)
2. being accused of lying (al-ittihām bi al-kidhb)
3. open sin (fisq)
4. being unknown (jahālah)
5. innovation (bidʿah)

Lying (al-kidhb): It is proven that the narrator has lied at least once regarding the aḥādīth of the Prophet ﷺ.

Suspicion of lying (al-ittihām bi al-kidhb): Meaning the person has a reputation of telling lies even if he is not specifically known to have lied concerning a ḥadīth.

Open Sin (Fisq): Sinful conduct especially in public, which was considered to be a sign of shamelessness.

Being Unknown (Jahālah): The narrator is unknown in terms of identification or uprightness. This is not in regards to the narrator themself, but rather in the sense of them being considered a link in the chain.

Innovation (Bidʿah): Having views and beliefs that are contrary to well-known beliefs.

Al-Ḍabṭ can be understood to be accuracy. It refers to the narrator's ability to listen to a ḥadīth, understand its meaning, retain it, and pass it on just as they heard it. The ḍabṭ of a narrator is determined through corroboration. There are five factors that are considered to negatively affect the ḍabṭ of a narrator:

1. neglect/oversight (ghaflah)
2. frequent errors (fuḥsh al-ghalaṭ)
3. disagreement with reliable authorities and narrators (mukhālafah al-thiqāt)
4. known for misunderstandings (wahm)
5. bad memory (sūʾ al-ḥifẓ)

PART 2:

HADITH TERMINOLOGY

Part One of this booklet dealt with a very brief introduction to some of the various topics that are covered within Ḥadīth Studies. Part Two will shift gears and focus on a branch of Ḥadīth Studies known as Muṣṭalaḥ al-Ḥadīth, or Ḥadīth Terminology. Muṣṭalaḥ al-Ḥadīth focuses on the technical terms, names, and phrases that have developed over time that are used primarily to classify and categorize aḥādīth. The terminology that has been developed is quite specific and oftentimes a single word can convey multiple pieces of information. For example, amongst scholars and students of ḥadīth the use of words such as musnad, muttaṣil, marfūʿ, mursal, maqṭuʿ, munqaṭiʿ, and ṣaḥīḥ covey full identification of the type of ḥadīth and relative strength and weakness of its chain. Studying these different terms and what they mean is extremely important for any student of ḥadīth and for anyone who wants to have a solid understanding of ḥadīth literature.

CLASSIFICATION OF HADITH

A ḥadīth can be analyzed and classified through many different angles or perspectives. For example, aḥādīth can be classified with respect to its sanad (chain) and matn (text). Aḥādīth are commonly classified according to the following five perspectives:

1. authority
2. number of narrators
3. authenticity
4. continuity
5. breaks

8

CLASSIFICATION OF HADITH ACCORDING TO AUTHORITY

This classification is based on the question: who actually said the statement or to whom is the statement attributed. The purpose of this classification is simply to identify its origin or its source; meaning, who actually said it? Was it the Prophet ﷺ, a Companion, or even a Successor? This classification appeared early in Islamic history in order to clearly distinguish the statements of the Prophet ﷺ from those of his companions or their students.

Based on authority the scholars of ḥadīth have classified narrations into four categories:

1. al-Ḥadīth al-Qudsī
2. al-Ḥadīth al-Marfūʿ
3. al-Ḥadīth al-Mawqūf
4. al-Ḥadīth al-Maqṭūʿ

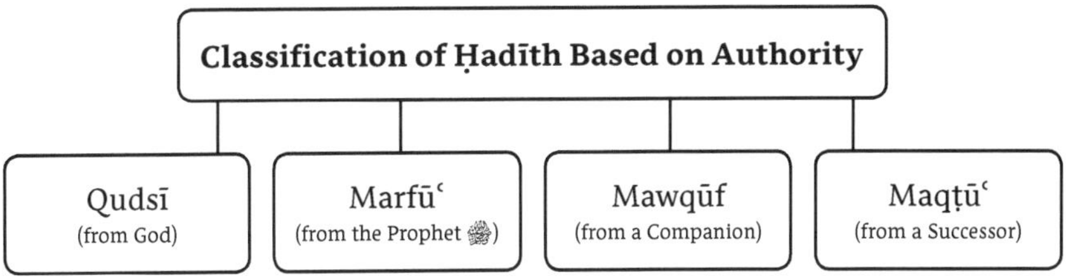

AL-HADITH AL-QUDSI: THE DIVINE HADITH

This is a narration whose chain ends at Allah ﷻ. It is a narration from the Prophet ﷺ attributed to Allah ﷻ. An easier way to describe it is a ḥadīth the Prophet ﷺ narrated from Allah ﷻ. That is why it is called qudsī, which comes from the word quds, which means holiness, sanctity, or purity. The term literally translates as the divine narration. Technically it is defined as a saying of the Prophet ﷺ that he ﷺ attributes to Allah ﷻ.

ما أضيف إلى رسول الله ﷺ و أسنده إلى ربه عز و جل

A ḥadīth qudsī is usually narrated in the following two ways:

1. The Prophet ﷺ said from amongst the sayings he ﷺ has narrated from his Lord, that God ﷻ said…

قال رسول الله ﷺ فيما يروى عن ربه

2. Allah ﷻ has said in what is narrated by the Prophet ﷺ…

قال الله تعالى فيما رواه عنه رسول الله ﷺ

Example:

وعن أبي هريرة رضى الله عنه، قال: قال رسول الله صلى الله عليه وسلم : "قال الله عز وجل: كل عمل ابن آدم له إلا الصيام، فإنه لى وأنا أجزى به. والصيام جُنة فإذا كان يوم صوم أحدكم فلا يرفث ولا يصخب، فإن سابه أحد أو قاتله، فليقل: إنى صائم. والذى نفس محمد بيده لخُلوف فم الصائم أطيب عند الله من ريح المسك. "للصائم فرحتان يفرحهما: إذا أفطر فرح بفطره، وإذا لقى ربه فرح بصومه"
((متفق عليه))

Abū Hurayrah رضي الله عنه narrated that the Messenger of Allah ﷺ said, "Allah the Exalted and Majestic said: 'Every act of the son of Adam is for him, except fasting. It is (exclusively) meant for Me and I (alone) will reward it. Fasting is a shield. When any one of you is fasting on a day, he should neither indulge in obscene language, nor raise the voice; or if anyone reviles him or tries to quarrel with him, he should say: I am a person fasting. By Him, in Whose Hand is the life of Muhammad, the breath of the observer of fast is sweeter to Allah on the Day of Judgment than the fragrance of musk. The one who fasts has two (occasions) of joy, one when he breaks the fast he is glad with the breaking of (the fast) and one when he meets his Lord he is glad with his fast.'"[48]

Generally speaking, the subject matter of a ḥadīth qudsī will deal with virtues and rewards. There are not that many ḥadīth qudsī recorded in ḥadīth literature, approximately 200 or so. Similarly not all ḥadīth qudsī are authentic. They are subject to the same critique as any other ḥadīth so they can be authentic, good, or weak.

DIFFERENCE BETWEEN AL-HADITH AL-QUDSI AND THE QURAN

When talking about ḥadīth qudsī a natural question that arises is what is the difference between a ḥadīth qudsī and the Quran? Aren't they both from Allah ﷻ? The main or primary difference between the Quran and a ḥadīth qudsī is that the Quran was revealed both in terms of words and meanings; whereas, in a ḥadīth qudsī, the words are those of the Prophet ﷺ but the meanings are inspired by Allah ﷻ.

One of the scholars wrote, "Both the words and meanings of the Quran are from Allah ﷻ through manifest revelation. As for the ḥadīth qudsī then its wording is from the Prophet ﷺ and its meaning is from Allah ﷻ through inspiration or a dream."[49] Another way of expressing it is that the Quran is the eternal uncreated speech of Allah ﷻ revealed to the Prophet ﷺ through the Angel Jibrīl عليه السلام. As for a ḥadīth qudsī, Allah ﷻ inspires the Prophet ﷺ with its meaning and the Prophet ﷺ expresses it in his own words.

The following are considered to be some of the main differences between the Quran and ḥadīth qudsī:

48 al-Bukhārī, *k. al-ṣawm, b. hal yaqūlu innī ṣā'im idhā shutima*, 1904

49 'Itr, *Manhaj al-Naqd fī 'Ulūm al-Ḥadīth*, p.324

1. The Quran is miraculous. It is the inimitable, miraculous, divine, eternal, uncreated speech of Allah ﷻ, whereas, a ḥadīth qudsī is the speech of the Prophet ﷺ used to express meanings inspired to him directly from Allah ﷻ.
2. Reciting the words of the Quran is an act of worship that is rewarded; it is recited in prayer, cannot be touched by a person in the state of minor ritual impurity, and it cannot be recited by one in a state of major ritual impurity. None of these apply to a ḥadīth qudsī.
3. The Quran is mutawātir; a transmission is called mutawātir when it is reported by such a large number of people that they could not intentionally or mistakenly agree upon a lie. In each generation so many people narrated it that there is no question of its authenticity. The same cannot be said for the vast majority of ḥadīth qudsī.

AL-HADITH AL-MARFU': THE ELEVATED HADITH

Linguistically the word marfūʿ is the passive participle from the verb rafaʿa (رفع), which means to raise, lift, or elevate. The word marfūʿ - in its literal sense - means elevated. Technically, al-ḥadīth al-marfūʿ is defined as a saying, action, tacit approval, or characteristic directly and explicitly attributed to the Prophet ﷺ.

ما أضيف إلى النبي ﷺ من قول أو فعل أو تقرير أو صفة

In other words it is what has been narrated on the authority of the Prophet ﷺ in terms of his actions, sayings, tacit approvals, and characteristics. It is the exact same definition as for the word ḥadīth.

From this definition scholars have categorized marfūʿ aḥādīth into four types:

1. **Statements (al-marfūʿ al-qawlī):** These are aḥādīth that are narrated using the words "I heard the Prophet ﷺ saying such and such", "The Messenger of Allah ﷺ said" or "from the Messenger of Allah ﷺ".

   Example: ʿUmar (رضي الله عنه) narrated that I heard the Prophet ﷺ

saying, "Indeed actions are only by their intentions."[50]

2. **Action (al-marfūʿ al-fiʿlī):** Narrations that are talking about the actions of the Prophet ﷺ. They are narrated using the words "I saw the Prophet ﷺ do such and such", or "from the Prophet ﷺ that he did such and such."
3. **Tacit Approval (al-marfūʿ al-taqrīrī):** The word taqrīr, literally means approval, and it refers to the approval of the Prophet ﷺ. Meaning, someone said or did something in the presence of the Prophet ﷺ and he ﷺ did not object to it or prohibit it. Rather, he remained silent as a sign of approval.
4. **Moral Character/Physical Description (al-marfūʿ al-waṣfī):** Narrations describing the noble characteristics of the Prophet ﷺ or his physical description.

   Examples: "The Prophet ﷺ was the most generous of people and he would be the most generous in Ramaḍān."[51] Jābir (رضي الله عنه) narrated, "I once saw the Messenger of Allah ﷺ on the night of a full moon. On that night he wore red clothing. I would glance back and forth between the full moon and the Messenger of Allah ﷺ, and ultimately I came to the conclusion that the Messenger of Allah ﷺ was more handsome, beautiful and more radiant than the full moon."[52]

A marfūʿ ḥadīth is also subject to the same investigation and criticism as other narrations; so it can be authentic, good, or even weak.

AL-HADITH AL-MAWQUF: THE SUSPENDED HADITH

Linguistically, the word mawqūf is the passive participle from the verb waqafa (وقف), which means to stop. The word mawqūf means something that is stopped, halted, or suspended. Technically, al-ḥadīth al-mawqūf is a statement, action or tacit approval attributed to a Companion رضي الله عنه.

ما أضيف إلى الصحابي من قول أو فعل أو تقرير

50 al-Bukhārī, *k. bad' al-waḥyī, b. kayfa kāna bad' al-waḥyī ilā rasūlillah*, 1

51 al-Bukhārī, *k. al-ṣawm, b. ajwadu mā kāna al-nabiyy ﷺ yakūnu fī ramaḍān*, 1902

52 al-Tirmidhī, *shamā'il, b. mā jā'a fī khalq rasūlillāh ﷺ*, 9

Meaning the chain of narrators, the isnād, stops at the Companion. The statement, action or tacit approval is that of the companion.

From this definition scholars categorize a mawqūf ḥadīth into three types:

1. **Statement (al-mawqūf al-qawlī):** ʿAli ibn Abī Ṭālib ﵁ said, "Speak to the people with what they know. Would you like for Allah and His Messenger ﷺ to be rejected?"[53]

قال علي بن أبي طالب رضى الله عنه، حدثوا الناس بما
يعرفون أتحبون أن يكذب الله و رسوله؟

2. **Action (al-mawqūf al-fiʿlī):** "Ibn ʿAbbās ﵄ led prayer with tayammum (dry ablution)."[54]
3. **Tacit Approval (al-mawqūf al-taqrīrī):** If some Successor said, "I did such and such in the presence of a Companion and he didn't disapprove."

Sometimes there are narrations that are mawqūf in terms of their isnād and wording as well; however, after further investigation it can be understood that some ḥadīth mawqūf are actually marfūʿ. The scholars of ḥadīth have developed some general guidelines to determine which mawqūf narrations are actually considered to be marfūʿ. For example, if a companion who is not known to have taken from Judeo-Christian narrations, narrated something that has no room for one's personal opinion or understanding it is considered to be marfūʿ; meaning they must have heard it from the Prophet ﷺ. This includes information about events from the past such as the beginning of creation or events from the future like signs of the Day of Judgment. Similarly, if a Companion does something that has no room for one's personal opinion or understanding it will be considered to be marfūʿ. For example, when ʿAli ﵁ prayed the prayer of eclipse while bowing down twice in each unit. It is not feasible to think that ʿAlī ﵁ would do something like this if he didn't learn it from the Prophet ﷺ.

---

53 al-Bukhārī, *k. al-ʿilm*, 49

54 al-Bukhārī, *k. al-tayammum, b. al-ṣaʿīd al-ṭayyib waḍūʾ al-muslim*

AL-HADITH AL-MAQTU': THE SEVERED (CUT-OFF) HADITH

Linguistically, the word maqṭūʿ is the passive participle from the Arabic verb qaṭaʿa (قطع), which means to cut or sever. The word maqṭūʿ literally means something that has been cut-off or severed. Technically, it refers to a saying or action attributed to a Successor ﷺ (someone who saw a Companion but did not see The Prophet ﷺ).

ما أضيف إلى التابعى أو من دونه من قول أو فعل

This is a narration that transmits the statement or action of one of the Successors. For example, al-Ḥasan al-Baṣrī ﷺ said regarding praying behind an innovator, "Pray and his innovation is upon him."[55]

قال الحسن البصرى، صل وعليه بدعته

Another example is the statement of Masrūq ibn al-Ajdaʿ who said, "It is sufficient for a person to be considered a scholar if he fears Allah and for a person to be ignorant if he boasts with his knowledge."[56]

عن مسروق قال، كفى بالمرء علما أن يخشى الله وكفى بالمرء
جهلا أن يعجب بعلمه

Another example is that it has been narrated that Masrūq ﷺ would draw a curtain between him and his family, turn towards prayer and leave them and their affairs."[57]

كان مسروق يرخى الستر بينه وبين أهله ويقبل على صلاته
ويخليهم ودنياهم

---

55 al-Bukhārī, *k. al-adhān, b. imāmah al-maftūn wa al-mubtadiʿ*

56 al-Dāramī, 319 and 389

57 Abū Naʿīm, *Hilyah al-Awliyāʾ*, 1652

9

CLASSIFICATION OF HADITH ACCORDING TO THE NUMBER OF NARRATORS

This is a classification that is based upon the number of narrators at each level of the chain or the isnād. It literally looks at the number of narrators at the first level, the second level, the third level and so on until it reaches the compiler of a major collection. Depending on the number of narrators at each level of the chain of narration (isnād) aḥādīth are classified into two broad categories:

1. mutawātir
2. āḥād

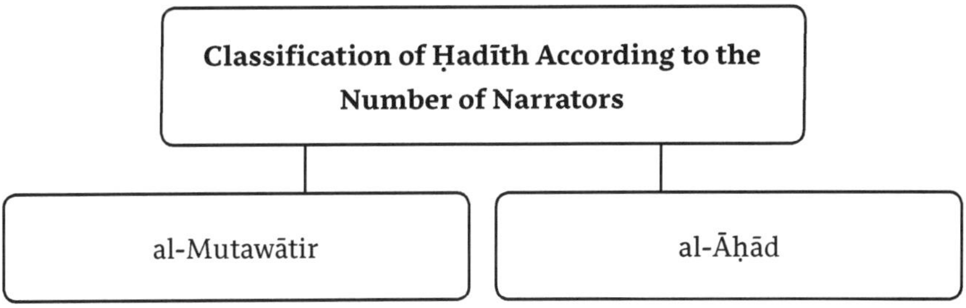

AL-HADITH AL-MUTAWATIR: THE CONSECUTIVELY RECURRENT HADITH

Linguistically, the word mutawātir is the active participle from the verb tawātara (تواتر), which means to follow in uninterrupted succession, to repeat itself, continue regularly, uninterruptedly; or to be uninterrupted, or unbroken. The word mutawātir is translated as consecutively recurrent. Technically, it is a ḥadīth that has been narrated by such a large number of people that it is inconceivable that they would have all collaborated in order to perpetuate a lie.

ما رواه عدد كثير تحيل العادة تواطؤهم على الكذب

Meaning at every single level of the chain, in every generation, there were so many people who narrated the ḥadīth that it is impossible for them to have agreed upon a lie intentionally or unintentionally. The possibility of this report being false or weak is impossible because of the large number of narrators and the diversity of localities. This large number of narrators is enough to declare the report or the ḥadīth to be authentic; it is above criticism. If a ḥadīth is mutawātir its narrators will not be subject to evaluation to see if they were upright and accurate. This is because in a mutawātir ḥadīth credibility is given solely to the multitude and number of narrators. A mutawātir ḥadīth gives the benefit of certainty. One can be absolutely, 100% certain that this is a statement of the Prophet ﷺ.

From this definition the scholars of ḥadīth say that in order for a ḥadīth to be considered mutawātir four conditions must be met:

1. Numerous Narrators: The ḥadīth must be narrated by a large number of narrators at each level of the chain; from the beginning until the end. The problem that arises here is that there is no consensus amongst ḥadīth scholars regarding what exactly that "large" number is. There is no specified minimum or maximum number given. Some say the requirement is four, others 10, others 20, 40, 70 up to a few hundred. The basic premise behind the "large" number is to inspire certainty and conviction, and that cannot really be linked to a specific number. Certainty can sometimes be achieved by a

relatively small number. According to some ḥadīth scholars the most agreed upon number is 10. But as stated before, the central purpose is to ensure that this group of people, regardless of size, would not be able to collude upon a lie.

2. This "large" number of narrators must exist at each level of the chain. So if the number of narrators drops below this level at any point in the chain it will not be considered to be mutawātir.
3. The impossibility of all the narrators agreeing upon a lie. This is caused mainly by two things; the "large" number and the different localities of the narrators.
4. The basis of the report is sensory perception and not rational thought. What that essentially means is that the report is narrated by the narrators saying we heard, saw or felt such and such.

If a narration fulfills these four conditions it is considered to be mutawātir. A mutawātir ḥadīth conveys certainty that is not open to challenge or doubt and the ruling that is established by it is definitive. As a side note, this is how the Quran has been narrated from generation to generation in addition to being preserved through writing.

TYPES OF MUTAWATIR

Mutawātir Aḥādīth are classified into the following two categories:

1. AL-MUTAWĀTIR AL-LAFẒĪ (MUTAWĀTIR IN WORDING):

This term refers to a mutawātir ḥadīth that consists of the verbatim transmission of the sayings of the Prophet ﷺ. Meaning these are the exact words spoken by the Prophet ﷺ.

ما تواتر لفظه و معناه

For example, the Prophet ﷺ said, "Whoever tells a lie upon me intentionally then let them prepare their seat in the Hellfire."[58]

58 al-Bukhārī, *k. al-ʿilm, b. ithm man kadhaba ʿalā al-nabiyy* ﷺ, 107

عَنْ أَبِي سَعِيدٍ قَالَ: قَالَ رَسُولُ اللَّهِ ـ صلى الله عليه وسلم ـ "مَنْ كَذَبَ عَلَيَّ مُتَعَمِّدًا فَلْيَتَبَوَّأْ مَقْعَدَهُ مِنَ النَّارِ"

This ḥadīth has been narrated by a number of Companions ﷺ including ʿAli, al-Zubayr ibn al-ʿAwwām, Anas ibn Mālik, Salamah, and Abū Hurayrah ﷺ. Other Companions ﷺ narrated it from them, and then their students, and their students, and so on.

The scholars of ḥadīth have differed with respect to the existence and scope of this type of narration. For example, some ḥadīth scholars claimed that such a ḥadīth does not exist and others said that they are rare. However, the vast majority of scholars such as Ibn Ḥajar al-ʿAsqalānī, Ibn Ḥazm al-Ẓāhirī, Qāḍī ʿIyāḍ, and Jalāl al-Dīn al-Suyūṭī maintain that these type of mutawātir narrations are not rare.

Jalāl al-Dīn al-Suyūṭī ﷺ authored a book entitled *al-Azhār al-Mutanāthira fī al-Akhbār al-Mutawātirah* (Scattered Flowers within Mutawātir Reports), which he later summarized in *Qatf al-Azhār* (Plucking the Flowers) in which he tried to compile a number of mutawātir aḥādīth. Within this collection the author considers the following aḥādīth to be mutawātir:

1. "Every intoxicant is wine and all wine is forbidden."[59]

   كل مسكر خمر و كل خمر حرام

2. "May Allah cause to flourish a slave (of His) who hears my words and understands them, and then he conveys them from me. There are those who have knowledge but no understanding, and there may be those who convey knowledge to those who may have more understanding of it than they do."[60]

   نَضَّرَ اللَّهُ عَبْدًا سَمِعَ مَقَالَتِي فَوَعَاهَا ثُمَّ بَلَّغَهَا عَنِّي فَرُبَّ حَامِلِ فِقْهٍ غَيْرِ فَقِيهٍ وَرُبَّ حَامِلِ فِقْهٍ إِلَى مَنْ هُوَ أَفْقَهُ مِنْهُ

59 Muslim, *k. al-ashribah, b. bayān anna kulla muskir khamr wa anna kulla khamr ḥarām*, 2003
60 al-Tirmidhī, *k. al-ʿilm ʿan rasūlillah* ﷺ, *b. mā jāʾa fī al-hath ʿalā tablīgh al-samāʿi*, 2658

3. "Everyone will find easy that which they have been created for."[61]

كل ميسر لما خلق له

Al-Bukhārī and Muslim have recorded other aḥādīth that are considered to be mutawātir as well. For example, "The Prophet ﷺ wiped over his leather socks."[62] This ḥadīth has been narrated by approximately eighty Companions of the Prophet ﷺ. Other examples are the famous ḥadīth about seeing Allah ﷻ in the hereafter and the basin of the Prophet ﷺ in the hereafter.

2. *AL-MUTAWĀTIR AL-MAʿNAWĪ (MUTAWĀTIR IN MEANING):*

A ḥadīth that is mutawātir in meaning is one in which the wording of the ḥadīth itself may not be mutawātir, but there are so many other narrations that talk about the same thing, subject, topic, or meaning that it is considered to be mutawātir. It is when a number of aḥādīth share the same subject or meaning, but the wording of each individual report is not mutawātir.

ما تواتر معناه دون لفظه

An example of this is all the various aḥādīth that have been narrated regarding raising one's hands at the time of supplication. There are a number of aḥādīth that confirm this, and although each one of these if taken individually would not be mutawātir, the common theme becomes mutawātir. There are literally almost a 100 aḥādīth that confirm this.

A theoretical example that might help understand this concept is that of a fire downtown. One person might report that they saw smoke coming out of a building. Another report might say that there were people running away from downtown. Another report might say that there were fire trucks rushing towards downtown. Someone else might report that they saw helicopters and another one might say they saw flames. When all of these reports are put together they support a common theme, which is a fire downtown.

This type of tawātur is established for a number of acts of worship such as the way to perform wuḍū', how the imām leads ṣalāh, and how ḥajj should be performed.

61 al-Bukhārī, *k. al-tawḥīd, b. qawlillah wa laqad yassarna al-Quran li al-dhikr*, 7551

62 Muslim, *k. al-ṭahārah, b. al-masḥ ʿalā al-khuffayn*, 274

KHABAR AL-AHAD: THE SOLITARY REPORT

The second type of ḥadīth with respect to the number of narrators is called khabar al-āḥād. It is also known as khabar al-wāḥid. Linguistically, the word āḥād is the plural of wāḥid, which means one and singular. Technically, it is defined as a narration that does not fulfill the conditions of a mutawātir narration.

هو ما لم يجمع شروط المتواتر

It is a ḥadīth that does not fulfill all the conditions necessary for it to be considered mutawātir. It might be narrated by one, two, three or even more narrators at each level of the chain, but it does not reach that "large" number required for it to be mutawātir.

The vast majority of aḥādīth that are found in the ḥadīth corpus are all āḥād. The āḥād narrations are subject to criticism; these are the aḥādīth whose narrators are evaluated for uprightness and accuracy to determine if the narration is authentic or not. The scholars of ḥadīth classify the āḥād narrations with respect to two different considerations:

1. with respect to the number of narrators
2. with respect to authenticity

The āḥād narrations give the benefit of near certain knowledge and can be used to derive legal rulings. Individually transmitted reports make action obligatory, but do not make knowledge obligatory. The various schools of thought have developed different principles for accepting and acting upon āḥād narrations. Meaning, just because a ḥadīth is authentic does not necessarily mean that it is acted upon as well. For example, the scholars of the ḥanafī school of thought have established certain conditions that a āḥād ḥadīth must fulfill in order for it to be considered a proof and a basis for action. One of them is that the companion narrator of the āḥād narration is not known to have acted against it themselves. If it is known that the narrator acted against his or her own report that means that they must have heard or learnt something else from the Prophet ﷺ as well. That is why the ḥanafīs do not act upon the ḥadīth of Abū Hurayrah ﵁ in which he narrated that the Prophet ﷺ said, "When a dog licks a dish wash it seven times, one of them with pure dirt."[63] Because Abū Hurayrah ﵁ himself would give the fatwā (religious verdict) that it only needed to be washed three times.

Another condition is that the content of the ḥadīth should not be something that necessitates (ʿumūm al-balwā) the knowledge of a large number of people. If that is the case, then it would be expected that more than just a handful of people would have narrated that ḥadīth. For example, the Prophet ﷺ said, "If one of you touches his private part then they should make wuḍūʾ."[64] This ḥadīth is only narrated by one female Companion. Seeing as though touching one's private parts is something that all the Companions would have experienced, it logically follows that at least a handful of Companions would narrate and talk about this. Because they did not, we can say that this is an āḥād narration, and therefore it does not carry the same legal weight as the mutawātir narrations on the same topic.

63 Muslim, *k. al-ṭahārah, b. ḥukm wulūgh al-kalb*, 279

64 al-Nasāʾī, *k. al-ghasl wa al-tayammum, b. al-wuḍūʾ min mas al-dhakr*, 445

10

TYPES OF AHAD ACCORDING TO NUMBER OF NARRATORS

According to the number of narrators at each level of the chain the scholars of ḥadīth classify āḥād narrations as:

1. al-Mashhūr
2. al-ʿAzīz
3. al-Gharīb

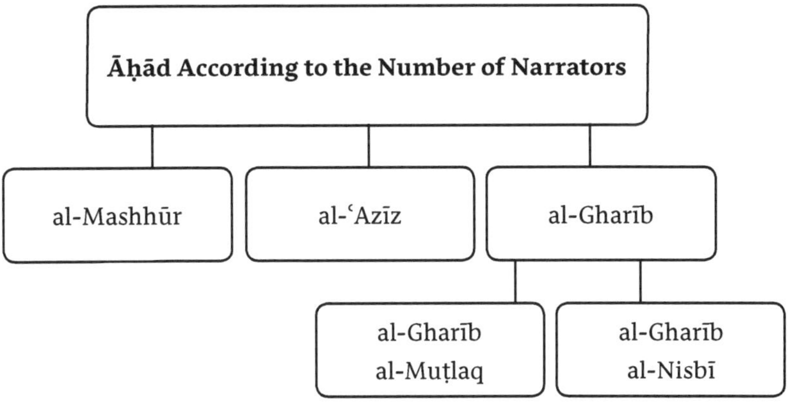

AL-MASHHUR (THE WELL-KNOWN)

Linguistically, the word mashhūr is the passive participle from the verb shahara (شهر), which means to make well-known, famous, or widespread. The word mashhūr literally means well-known, famous, or widespread. Technically, a mashhūr narration is defined as a ḥadīth with at least three narrators at every link in the chain or isnād.

مَا رَوَاهُ ثَلَاثَةٌ فَأَكْثَرَ فِي كُلِّ طَبَقَةٍ، مَا لَمْ يَبلُغْ حَدَّ التَّوَاتُرِ

In each generation there are at least three or more people narrating the ḥadīth. If at any point in the chain there are less than three narrators then it will not be classified as mashhūr.

Example:

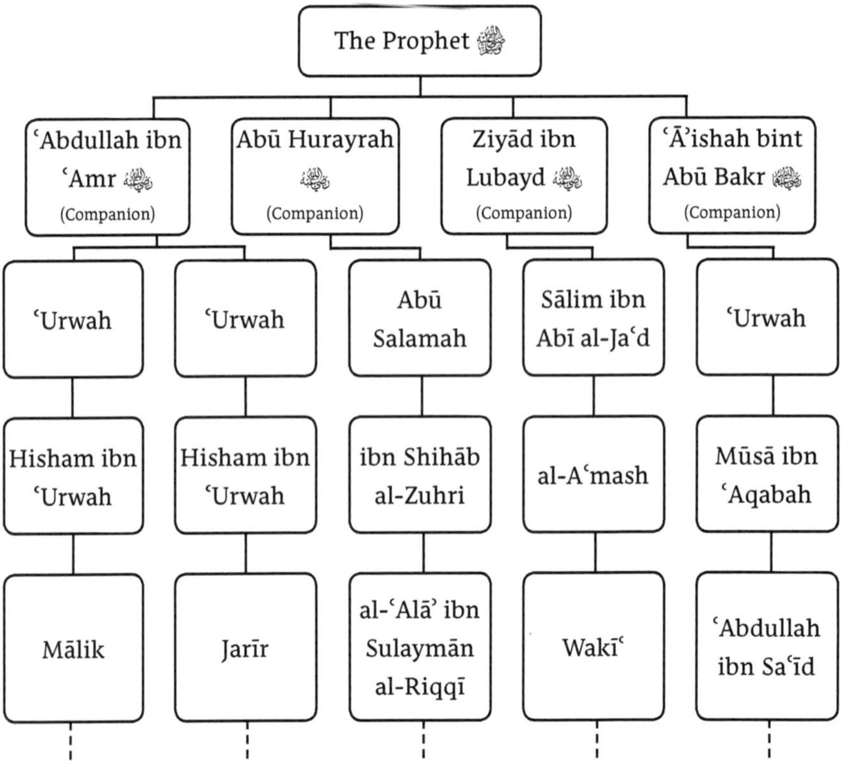

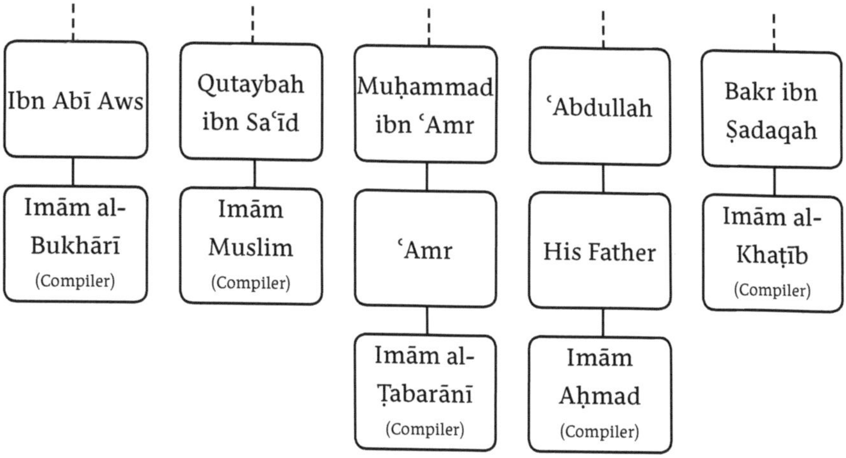

حَدَّثَنَا إِسمَاعِيلُ بنُ أَبِي أُوَيسٍ قَالَ حَدَّثَنِي مَالِكٌ، عَن هِشَامِ بنِ عُروَةَ، عَن أَبِيهِ، عَن عَبدِ اللَّهِ بنِ عَمرِو بنِ العَاصِ، قَالَ سَمِعتُ رَسُولَ اللَّهِ صَلَّى اللَّهُ عَلَيهِ وَسَلَّمَ يَقُولُ: "إِنَّ اللَّهَ لاَ يَقبِضُ العِلمَ انتِزَاعًا، يَنتَزِعُهُ مِنَ العِبَادِ، وَلَكِن يَقبِضُ العِلمَ بِقَبضِ العُلَمَاءِ، حَتَّى إِذَا لَم يُبقِ عَالِمًا، اتَّخَذَ النَّاسُ رُءُوسًا جُهَّالاً فَسُئِلُوا، فَأَفتَوا بِغَيرِ عِلمٍ، فَضَلُّوا وَأَضَلُّوا

Ismāʿīl ibn Abī Uwais narrated to us, who said that Mālik narrated to him from Hishām ibn ʿUrwah from his father, from ʿAbdullāh ibn ʿAmr ibn al-ʿĀṣ (رضي الله عنهما), who said I heard the Messenger of Allah ﷺ saying, "Verily, Allah does not take away knowledge by snatching it from the people but He takes away knowledge by taking away the scholars, so that when He leaves no learned person, people turn to the ignorant as their leaders; then they are asked to deliver religious verdicts and they deliver them without knowledge, they go astray, and lead others astray."[65]

It is important to note that a mashhūr narration must have become well-known and widespread during the first three generations of Islam. Following that period most aḥādīth became widespread and well-known. A mashhūr ḥadīth is also subject to critique and evaluation; it can be ṣaḥīḥ, ḥasan, or

65 al-Bukhārī, *k. al-ʿilm*, *b. kayfa yuqbaḍu al-ʿilm*, 100

even ḍaʿīf depending on the condition of its narrators in the isnād.

NON-TECHNICAL MASHHŪR

A non-technical mashūr is a narration that has become well-known, famous, and widespread even though it may not fit the technical definition. The spread of a ḥadīth is a relative concept to some extent in that a ḥadīth may be well-known in some areas but not in others. For example, a ḥadīth maybe widespread among the fuqahāʾ (jurists), the scholars of ḥadīth, scholars of uṣūl, or just the masses. If a ḥadīth is well-known in its literal sense without meeting the conditions of the ḥadīth scholars it is called a non-technical mashhūr.

An example is the well-known ḥadīth that the Prophet ﷺ said, "Patient deliberation is from Allah ﷻ and hastiness is from Satan."[66]

الأناة من الله والعجلة من الشيطان

Another famous ḥadīth amongst the jurists is, "Divorce is the most detestable of all permissible things to Allah ﷻ."[67]

أبغض الحلال إلى الله الطلاق

AL-AZIZ (THE STRONG HADITH)

Linguistically, the word ʿazīz is derived from the verb ʿazza - yaʿizzu (عزا يعِزُّ), which means to become rare or scarce or from the verb ʿazza - yaʿazzu (عزا يعَزُّ), which means to become strong. The word ʿazīz literally means something that is rare or something that is strong. Technically, an ʿazīz narration is a ḥadīth that has at least two narrators at every level of the chain.

ما لا يقل رواته عن اثنين فى جميع طبقات السند

It is a ḥadīth in which at least one link in its isnād only has two narrators, even if the other links have more than two. None of the links in the chain has

66 al-Tirmidhī, *k. al-birr wa al-ṣilah ʿan rasūlillah* ﷺ, *b. mā jāʾa fī al-taʾannī wa al-ʿajalah*, 2012

67 Abū Dāwūd, *k. al-ṭalāq, b. fī karāhiyyah al-ṭalāq*, 2178

less than two narrators. It is called ʿAzīz because it is both strong and scarce.

Example:

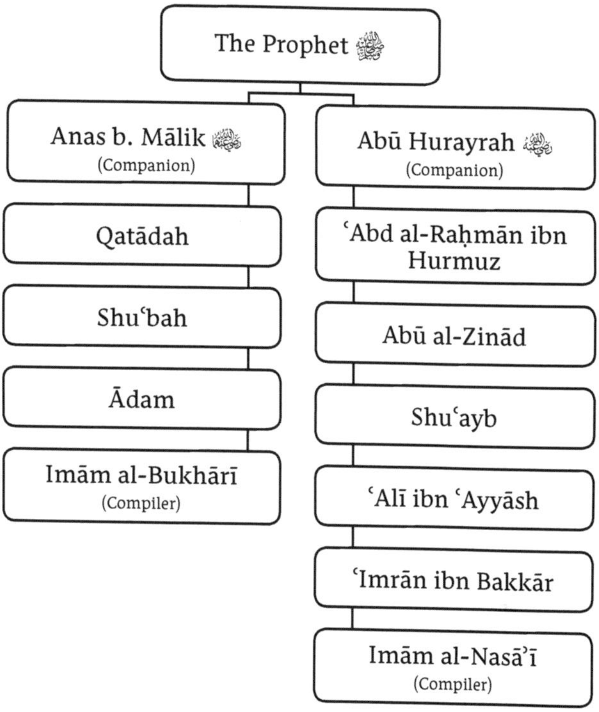

حَدَّثَنَا مُحَمَّدُ بْنُ الْمُثَنَّى، وَابْنُ بَشَّارٍ قَالاَ حَدَّثَنَا مُحَمَّدُ بْنُ جَعْفَرٍ،
حَدَّثَنَا شُعْبَةُ، قَالَ سَمِعْتُ قَتَادَةَ، يُحَدِّثُ عَنْ أَنَسِ بْنِ مَالِكٍ، قَالَ
قَالَ رَسُولُ اللَّهِ صلى الله عليه وسلم : "لاَ يُؤْمِنُ أَحَدُكُمْ حَتَّى
أَكُونَ أَحَبَّ إِلَيْهِ مِنْ وَلَدِهِ وَوَالِدِهِ وَالنَّاسِ أَجْمَعِينَ."

Muḥammad ibn al-Muthannā and ibn Bashār narrated to us, who said that Muḥammad ibn Jaʿfar narrated to us, who said that Shuʿbah narrated to us, who said I heard Qatādah narrating from Anas ibn Mālik ﵁, who said that the Messenger of Allah ﷺ said, "None of you truly believes until I'm more beloved to him than his child, his father and all of mankind."[68]

68 Muslim, *k. al-īmān*, *b. wujūb maḥabbah rasūlillah* ﷺ *akthar min al-ahl*, 44

An ʿazīz ḥadīth may be sound (ṣaḥīḥ), good (ḥasan), or weak (ḍaʿīf) depending on the reliability of its narrators.

AL-GHARIB (THE ISOLATED HADITH)

Linguistically, the word gharīb is an adjective that means strange or peculiar. Technically, a gharīb narration is a ḥadīth that is narrated by only one narrator at one link of the isnād.

ما ينفرد بروايته راو واحد

It is a narration that has a single narrator at any point in the isnād. This one narrator can be at any part of the chain; the beginning, middle, or end. The gharīb ḥadīth is classified into two types:

1. al-Gharīb al-Muṭlaq
2. al-Gharīb al-Nisbī

1. AL-GHARĪB AL-MUṬLAQ (ABSOLUTELY ISOLATED)

This is defined as a ḥadīth that has been narrated only by one Companion from the Prophet ﷺ, even if it became well-known and widely narrated at lower levels of the chain.

ما كانت الغرابة فى أصل سنده، أى ما ينفرد بروايته شخص واحد
فى أصل سنده

Example:

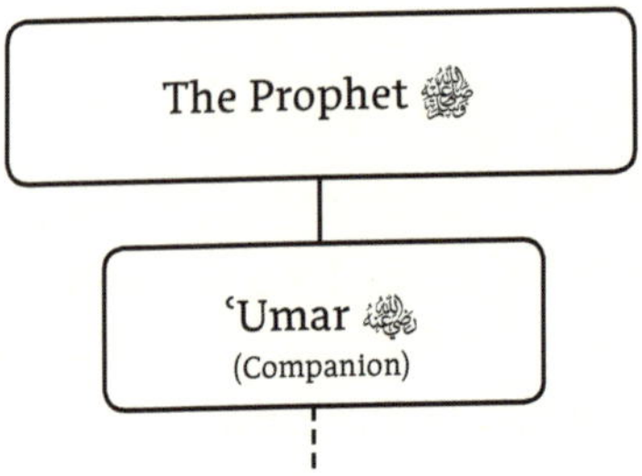

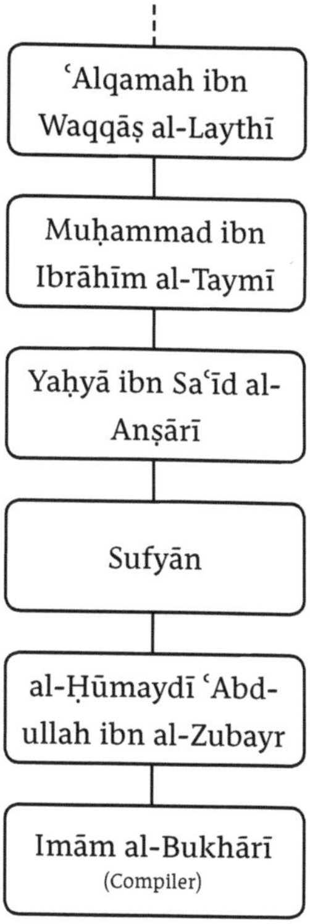

حَدَّثَنَا الْحُمَيْدِيُّ عَبْدُ اللَّهِ بْنُ الزُّبَيْرِ، قَالَ حَدَّثَنَا سُفْيَانُ، قَالَ
حَدَّثَنَا يَحْيَى بْنُ سَعِيدٍ الأَنْصَارِيُّ، قَالَ أَخْبَرَنِي مُحَمَّدُ بْنُ إِبْرَاهِيمَ
التَّيْمِيُّ، أَنَّهُ سَمِعَ عَلْقَمَةَ بْنَ وَقَّاصٍ اللَّيْثِيَّ، يَقُولُ سَمِعْتُ عُمَرَ بْنَ
الْخَطَّابِ ـ رضى الله عنه ـ عَلَى الْمِنْبَرِ قَالَ سَمِعْتُ رَسُولَ اللَّهِ صلى
الله عليه وسلم يَقُولُ : إِنَّمَا الأَعْمَالُ بِالنِّيَّاتِ، وَإِنَّمَا لِكُلِّ امْرِئٍ
مَا نَوَى، فَمَنْ كَانَتْ هِجْرَتُهُ إِلَى دُنْيَا يُصِيبُهَا أَوْ إِلَى امْرَأَةٍ يَنْكِحُهَا
فَهِجْرَتُهُ إِلَى مَا هَاجَرَ إِلَيْهِ

ʿUmar ibn al-Khaṭṭāb ﷺ narrated that he heard the Messenger of Allah ﷺ saying, "The reward of deeds depends upon the intentions and every person will get the reward according to what he has intended. So whoever emigrated for worldly benefits or for a woman to marry, his emigration was for what he emigrated for."[69]

This ḥadīth has only been narrated by ʿUmar ibn al-Khaṭṭāb.

2. *AL-GHARĪB AL-NISBĪ (RELATIVELY ISOLATED)*

This refers to a ḥadīth that has only one narrator at some other point in the chain. Meaning, more than one Companion narrated the ḥadīth from the Prophet, but then later on only a single narrated reported it.

Example:

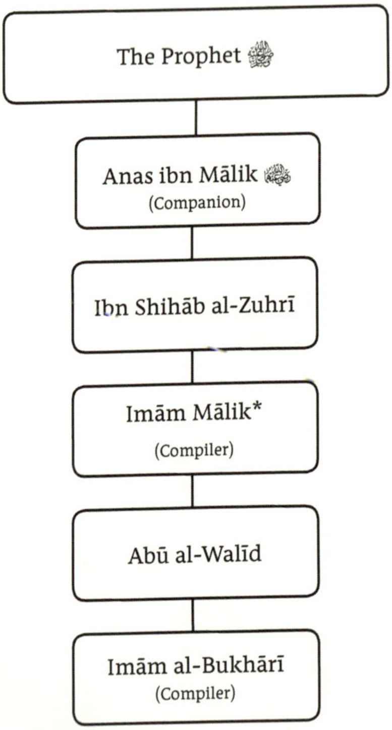

حَدَّثَنَا أَبُو الْوَلِيدِ، حَدَّثَنَا مَالِكٌ، عَنِ الزُّهْرِيِّ، عَنْ أَنَسٍ ـ رضى
الله عنه ـ أَنَّ النَّبِيَّ صلى الله عليه وسلم دَخَلَ مَكَّةَ عَامَ الْفَتْحِ
وَعَلَى رَأْسِهِ الْمِغْفَرُ

69 al-Bukhārī, *k. bada'a al-waḥy, b. kayfa kāna bad'u al-waḥy ilā rasūlillah*, 1

Abū al-Walīd narrated to us, who said that Mālik narrated to us, from al-Zuhrī from Anas ؓ that in the year of the conquest of Makkah the Prophet ﷺ entered Makkah, wearing a helmet on his head.[70]

Imām Mālik ؓ is the only student to have received this report from al-Zuhrī even though al-Zuhrī was a well-known scholar of ḥadīth with numerous students.

To reiterate, classifying a ḥadīth as mashhūr, ʿazīz, or gharīb does not imply its strength or weakness. The strength or weakness of a ḥadīth is dependent upon the reliability of the narrators found within its chain.

---

[70] al-Bukhārī, k. al-libās, b. al-mighfar, 5808

11

CLASSIFICATION OF AHAD WITH RESPECT TO STRENGTH & WEAKNESS

With respect to strength and weakness, meaning how reliable or unreliable the narration is, aḥādīth are initially divided into two broad categories: Accepted (Maqbūl) and Not Accepted (Mardūd). Accepted narrations are then classified into four categories according to the strength of their authenticity:

1. al-ṣaḥīḥ li dhātihi
2. al-ṣaḥīḥ li ghayrihi
3. al-ḥasan li dhātihi
4. al-ḥasan li ghayrihi

The Not Accepted report is termed as ḍaʿīf, or weak, which then has several types depending on what variable is causing the ḥadīth to be weak.

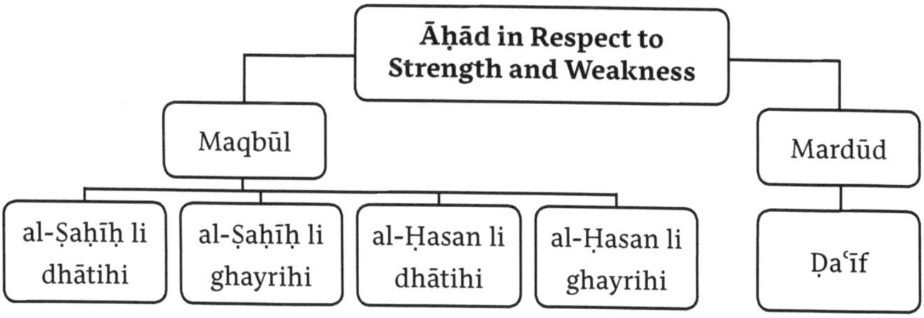

AL-SAHIH: THE AUTHENTIC HADITH

Al-Ḥadīth al-Ṣaḥīḥ is defined as a narration with a continuous chain of narrators all the way to the Prophet ﷺ, consisting of upright and accurate narrators that is not anomalous and free of defects.

ما اتصل سنده بنقل العدل الضابط عن مثله إلى منتهاه من غير
شذوذ و لا علة

From this definition we learn that in order for a ḥadīth to be considered authentic it must fulfill five conditions:

1. Continuity of the chain of narrators (اتصال السند): Meaning, the chain of narrators has to be connected all the way from the beginning until the Prophet ﷺ. Every narrator must have taken the ḥadīth directly from the narrator before them. The chain can not have any breaks or missing links anywhere. If the chain is broken at some point then the narration is automatically classified as weak.
2. Uprightness of the Narrators (العدالة): All the narrators must be upright; the scholars of ḥadīth usually define it as God-consciousness and good character. It refers to the narrator's moral character. It is an innate quality or nature (faculty) that causes a person to be God-conscious and well-mannered. God-consciousness (taqwā) is staying away from major sins and not being persistent in minor sins. The ʿadālah of a narrator is determined mostly through their biographical information. It is also dependent on their reputation and acceptance amongst other ḥadīth scholars. ʿAdālah was used to evaluate a narrator's character, belief, and level of piety.
3. Accuracy (الضبط): All the narrators in the chain must be known to have been accurate. It refers to the narrator's ability to listen to a ḥadīth, understand its meaning and to retain it, and pass it on just as they heard it. The ḍabṭ of a narrator is determined through corroboration. They must be accurate in terms of their memory as well as their written records.
4. Non Contradictory (عدم الشذوذ): Meaning the text of the ḥadīth can not be anomalous or unusual. The ḥadīth cannot contradict a reliable

ḥadīth reported by a larger number of narrators or even by one narrator of a higher authority or ranking.

5. Absence of Defects (عدم العلة): The ḥadīth has to be free from any type of defect whether apparent or hidden. A defect may exist in the chain of narrators or in the text itself. For example, there can be a break somewhere in the chain or there can be a mistake in the wording of the ḥadīth. All of these defects will be discussed later on in detail.

If a ḥadīth fulfills these five conditions it is considered to be authentic.

Example:

حَدَّثَنَا عَبْدُ اللَّهِ بْنُ يُوسُفَ، قَالَ أَخْبَرَنَا مَالِكٌ، عَنِ ابْنِ شِهَابٍ، عَنْ مُحَمَّدِ بْنِ جُبَيْرِ بْنِ مُطْعِمٍ، عَنْ أَبِيهِ، قَالَ سَمِعْتُ رَسُولَ اللَّهِ صلى الله عليه وسلم قَرَأَ فِي الْمَغْرِبِ بِالطُّورِ

ʿAbdullah ibn Yūsuf narrated to us, who said that Mālik informed us, from ibn Shihāb, from Muḥammad ibn Jubair ibn Muṭʿim, from his father who said, "I heard the Messenger of Allah ﷺ recite Surah al-Ṭūr in Maghrib."[71]

This ḥadīth is classified as ṣaḥīḥ because it fulfills all five of the conditions.

1. The chain is continuous. Each narrator is proven to be a student of the narrator above him.

2 & 3. All the narrators are upright and accurate:
- ʿAbdullāh ibn Yūsuf: trustworthy and accurate (thiqah/mutqin)
- Mālik ibn Anas: master of ḥadīth and accurate (imām/ḥāfiẓ)
- Ibn Shihāb al-Zuhrī: jurist and accurate agreed upon his magnificence and excellence (faqīh, ḥāfiẓ, muttafiq ʿalā jalālatihi wa itqānihi)
- Muḥammad ibn Jubayr: accurate (thiqah)
- Jubayr ibn Muṭʿim: A Companion.

4. The text of this ḥadīth does not contradict another authentic report.
5. There are no hidden or apparent defects.

71 al-Bukhārī, *k. al-adhān*, *b. al-jahr fī al-maghrib*, 765

THE MOST AUTHENTIC CHAINS OF NARRATION

When it comes to aḥādīth that are ṣaḥīḥ the scholars have tried to identify the most authentic chain of narrators or أصح الأسانيد. However, the reality is that no single chain can be declared to be the most authentic or the strongest because the level of authenticity of ṣaḥīḥ aḥādīth varies according to the relative strength of the five conditions.

Ibn al-Ṣalāḥ wrote, "The grades of sound ḥadīth vary in strength according to the degree that the ḥadīth possesses the aforementioned characteristics upon which soundness is based. In view of this, sound ḥadīth can be divided into subcategories. For this reason, we think that it is better to refrain from judging any chain of narration or ḥadīth to be the absolutely most sound. Although a number of ḥadīth authorities have attempted to do so."[72]

That is why some of the masters of ḥadīth identified certain chains to be the most authentic. For example, Isḥāq ibn Rāhawayh and Imām Aḥmad ibn Ḥanbal were of the opinion that the most reliable isnād is al-Zuhrī from Sālim from his father, ʿAbdullah ibn ʿUmar ﷺ. Ibn Maʿīn was of the opinion that the strongest chain is al-ʿAmash from Ibrāhīm al-Nakhaʿī from ʿAlqamah ibn Qays from ʿAbdullah ibn Masʿūd ﷺ. Imām al-Bukhārī was of the opinion that the strongest chain is Mālik from Nāfiʿ from ibn ʿUmar.

GRADES OR LEVELS OF AUTHENTIC HADITH

Ṣaḥīḥ is not a monolithic category of ḥadīth; meaning not every ḥadīth that is ṣaḥīḥ is equal in strength. There are different shades of ṣaḥīḥ, some being considered "stronger" than others. That is why the scholars have graded or classified ṣaḥīḥ ḥadīth into seven levels:

1. ṣaḥīḥ ḥadīth included in both al-Bukhārī and Muslim, which is termed "agreed upon" (متفق عليه).
2. ṣaḥīḥ ḥadīth included only in al-Bukhārī
3. ṣaḥīḥ ḥadīth included only in Muslim
4. ṣaḥīḥ ḥadīth that meet the conditions of authenticity of both al-Bukhārī and Muslim, but is not included in their collections.
5. ṣaḥīḥ ḥadīth that meets the standards of al-Bukhārī
6. ṣaḥīḥ ḥadīth that meets the standards of Muslim

72 ibn al-Ṣalāḥ, *An Introduction to the Science of the Hadith*, p. 5

7. ṣaḥīḥ ḥadīth that is graded as authentic by other ḥadīth scholars.

AL-HASAN: THE FAIR HADITH

Linguistically, the word ḥasan is an adjective that means beautiful, good, or nice. Technically, it is a narration that meets the conditions of a ṣaḥīḥ ḥadīth except that there is some weakness in the accuracy of one or a few of the narrators.

ما اتصل سنده بنقل العدل الذى خف ضبطه عن مثله إلى منتهاه
من غير شذوذ و لا علة

A narration with a continuous chain of narrators all the way to the Prophet ﷺ, consisting of upright and accurate narrators as well as one narrator (or more) with less accuracy that is not anomalous and free of defects. It meets the same conditions as a ṣaḥīḥ ḥadīth, except that one or more of its narrators' accuracy is of a lesser degree.

As mentioned earlier the accuracy (ḍabṭ) of a narrator is evaluated by comparing the reports of a particular narrator with similar reports by other more reliable narrators. When there is substantial corroboration, the ḍabṭ of the narrator is established, but if there is widespread discrepancy in the accuracy of his narrations the person will be considered to be weak. Again, it is the same thing as a ṣaḥīḥ ḥadīth except that one or more of its narrators has a lesser degree of accuracy. It can be thought of as a ḥadīth that falls in between ṣaḥīḥ and ḍaʿīf.

Example:

حَدَّثَنَا قُتَيْبَةُ، حَدَّثَنَا جَعْفَرُ بْنُ سُلَيْمَانَ الضُّبَعِيُّ، عَنْ أَبِي عِمْرَانَ
الْجَوْنِيِّ، عَنْ أَبِي بَكْرِ بْنِ أَبِي مُوسَى الأَشْعَرِيِّ، قَالَ سَمِعْتُ أَبِي
بِحَضْرَةِ الْعَدُوِّ، يَقُولُ قَالَ رَسُولُ اللَّهِ صلى الله عليه وسلم "إِنَّ
أَبْوَابَ الْجَنَّةِ تَحْتَ ظِلاَلِ السُّيُوفِ " . فَقَالَ رَجُلٌ مِنَ الْقَوْمِ رَثُّ
الْهَيْئَةِ أَأَنْتَ سَمِعْتَ هَذَا مِنْ رَسُولِ اللَّهِ صلى الله عليه وسلم

يَذْكُرُهُ قَالَ نَعَمْ . فَرَجَعَ إِلَى أَصْحَابِهِ فَقَالَ أَقْرَأُ عَلَيْكُمُ السَّلاَمَ .
وَكَسَرَ جَفْنَ سَيْفِهِ فَضَرَبَ بِهِ حَتَّى قُتِلَ

Qutaybah narrated to us, who said that Jaʿfar ibn Sulaymān al-Ḍubaʿī narrated to us, from Abū ʿImrān al-Jawnī, from Abū Bakr ibn Abī Mūsā al-Ashʿarī, who said I heard my father in the presence of the enemy saying, the Messenger of Allah ﷺ said, "Indeed, the gates of Paradise are under the shadows of the swords." A man among the people with ragged appearance said: "Have you heard what you mentioned from the Messenger of Allah ﷺ?" He said: "Yes." So he returned to his comrades and bid them farewell, broke the sheath of his sword, and began fighting with it until he was killed.[73]

The reason why this ḥadīth is graded as ḥasan is because all of the narrators in the chain are reliable (trustworthy), except for Jaʿfar ibn Sulaymān al-Ḍubaʿī who is graded as ḥasan al-ḥadīth. Meaning his accuracy is of a lesser level. The ḥadīth still meets the other four conditions:

1. continuity of the chain
2. uprightness of the narrators
3. not anomalous
4. no defects

A ḥasan ḥadīth is still considered to be a binding legal proof, just like a ṣaḥīḥ ḥadīth. Meaning it can be used to derive legal rulings.

AL-SAHIH LI GHAYRIHI (THE EXTRINSICALLY AUTHENTIC HADITH)

This is a narration that is considered to be authentic because of some extraneous evidence. It is a ḥasan ḥadīth that has been elevated to the level of ṣaḥīḥ because it is strengthened by multiple chains of narration.

هو الحسن لذاته إذا روى من طريق آخر مثله أو أقوى منه

73 al-Tirmidhī, k. *faḍāʾil al-jihād ʿan rasūlillah* ﷺ, b. *mā dhukira anna abwāb al-jannah taḥta dhilāl al-suyūf*, 1659

It has an unbroken chain of narrators all of whom are upright and accurate, it is not anomalous, and is free from defects. However, it contains a point of weakness because of the accuracy of one of its narrators. This weakness is made up for by the presence of another chain of narrators for the same ḥadīth in which all the narrators are upright and accurate.

Example:

حَدَّثَنَا أَبُو كُرَيْبٍ، حَدَّثَنَا عَبْدَةُ بْنُ سُلَيْمَانَ، عَنْ مُحَمَّدِ بْنِ عَمْرٍو، عَنْ أَبِي سَلَمَةَ، عَنْ أَبِي هُرَيْرَةَ، قَالَ قَالَ رَسُولُ اللَّهِ صلى الله عليه وسلم " لَوْلاَ أَنْ أَشُقَّ عَلَى أُمَّتِي لأَمَرْتُهُمْ بِالسِّوَاكِ عِنْدَ كُلِّ صَلاَةٍ "

Abū Kurayb narrated to us, who said that ʿAbdah ibn Sulaymān narrated to us, from Muḥammad ibn ʿAmr, from Abū Salamah, from Abū Hurayrah ؓ who said that the Messenger of Allah ﷺ said, "If it were not that it would be difficult on my nation, then I would have ordered them to use the siwāk (wooden tooth stick) for each prayer."[74]

Muḥammad ibn ʿAmr ibn ʿAlqamah is well-known for his truthfulness and piety but the scholars disagreed on his accuracy. He was known to have a weak memory. Based on that this narration by itself is graded as ḥasan. However, the exact same ḥadīth has been narrated through Muḥammad ibn Ibrāhīm from Abū Salamah from Zayd ibn Khālid from the Prophet ﷺ. Because of the existence of this narration, the previous one is raised from the status of ḥasan to ṣaḥīḥ li ghayrihī.

AL-DA'IF (THE WEAK HADITH)

Linguistically, the word ḍaʿīf means weak, the opposite of something strong. Technically, it is defined as a ḥadīth that does not meet the conditions of a ṣaḥīḥ or ḥasan ḥadīth.

ما لم يجمع صفة الحسن، بفقد شرط من شروطه

It is a ḥadīth in which any one or more of the five conditions of a ṣaḥīḥ

---

74   al-Tirmidhī, k. al-ṭahārah ʿan rasūlillāh ﷺ, b. mā jāʾa fī al-siwāk, 22

or ḥasan ḥadīth have not been met. The weakness may be in the chain, text or in both. For example, if the chain is broken at some point it is classified as weak. A ḥadīth will also be classified as weak if there are some issues with one or more of the narrators. There are two main reasons why a ḥadīth is considered to be weak:

1. problems in the chain
2. or problems with the narrators

There are many categories of weak aḥādīth. Depending on the weakness the narrations are given very specific names that indicate why they have been graded as weak. Aḥādīth that have been classified as weak because of problems with the narrators are classified as the following:

1. Matrūk (Renounced)
2. Munkar (Disclaimed)
3. Shādh (Anomalous)
4. Muʿallal (Defective)
5. Mudraj (Interpolated)
6. Maqlūb (Inverted)
7. Muḍṭarab (Perplexing)
8. Muṣaḥḥaf (Distorted)

Aḥādīth that are considered weak because of issues with the chain are classified into the following:

1. Muʿallaq (Hanging)
2. Mursal (Loose)
3. Muʿḍal (Problematic)
4. Munqaṭiʿ (Interrupted)
5. Mudallas (Hidden Defect)

Example:

حَدَّثَنَا سُوَيْدُ بْنُ سَعِيدٍ، حَدَّثَنَا أَبُو الأَحْوَصِ، عَنْ مُحَمَّدِ بْنِ

عُبَيْدِ اللَّهِ، عَنِ الْحَسَنِ بْنِ سَعْدٍ، عَنْ أَبِيهِ، عَنْ عَلِيٍّ، قَالَ جَاءَ رَجُلٌ إِلَى النَّبِيِّ ـ صلى الله عليه وسلم ـ فَقَالَ إِنِّي اغْتَسَلْتُ مِنَ الْجَنَابَةِ وَصَلَّيْتُ الْفَجْرَ ثُمَّ أَصْبَحْتُ فَرَأَيْتُ قَدْرَ مَوْضِعِ الظُّفْرِ لَمْ يُصِبْهُ الْمَاءُ . فَقَالَ رَسُولُ اللَّهِ ـ صلى الله عليه وسلم ـ "لَوْ كُنْتَ مَسَحْتَ عَلَيْهِ بِيَدِكَ أَجْزَأَكَ"

Suwaid ibn Saʿīd narrated to us, who said that Abū al-Aḥwaṣ narrated to us, from Muḥammad ibn ʿUbaydillah, from al-Ḥasan ibn Saʿd, from his father from ʿAlī ❀ who said, "A man came to the Prophet ❀ and said, "I bathed because of major ritual impurity, and I prayed fajr. Then I noticed a spot the size of a fingernail that the water did not reach." The Messenger of Allah ❀ said: "If you had wiped it that would have been sufficient for you."[75]

This ḥadīth is graded as ḍaʿīf because one or more of the narrators in this chain is considered to be weak. Some of the great scholars of ḥadīth criticism considered Muḥammad ibn ʿUbaydillah to be weak. For example, Ibn Ḥajar ❀ says that he is weak.

AL-ḤASAN LI GHAYRIHI (THE EXTRINSICALLY FAIR HADITH)

Al-Ḥasan li Ghayrihi is a ḍaʿīf ḥadīth that has been elevated to the status of ḥasan due to supporting narrations.

هو الضعيف إذا تعددت طرقه، ولم يكن سبب ضعفه فسق الراوي أو كذبه

The narration in itself is weak because of either a break in the chain or the weakness of a narrator. The weakness of the narrator can not be due to some deficiency in his uprightness like fisq (open sinning) or lying. However, there are other chains of transmission that are not defective for the same ḥadīth that strengthen it and elevate it to the status of ḥasan.

---

[75] Ibn Mājah, k. al-ṭahārah wa sunanuha, 664

Example:

حَدَّثَنَا مُحَمَّدُ بْنُ بَشَّارٍ، حَدَّثَنَا يَحْيَى بْنُ سَعِيدٍ، وَعَبْدُ الرَّحْمَنِ بْنُ مَهْدِيٍّ، وَمُحَمَّدُ بْنُ جَعْفَرٍ، قَالُوا حَدَّثَنَا شُعْبَةُ، عَنْ عَاصِمِ بْنِ عُبَيْدِ اللَّهِ، قَالَ سَمِعْتُ عَبْدَ اللَّهِ بْنَ عَامِرِ بْنِ رَبِيعَةَ، عَنْ أَبِيهِ، أَنَّ امْرَأَةً، مِنْ بَنِي فَزَارَةَ تَزَوَّجَتْ عَلَى نَعْلَيْنِ فَقَالَ رَسُولُ اللَّهِ صلى الله عليه وسلم " أَرَضِيتِ مِنْ نَفْسِكِ وَمَالِكِ بِنَعْلَيْنِ " . قَالَتْ نَعَمْ . قَالَ فَأَجَازَهُ

Muḥammad ibn Bashār narrated to us, who said that Yaḥyā ibn Saʿīd and ʿAbd al-Raḥmān ibn Mahdi and Muḥammad ibn Jaʿfar narrated to us, who all said that Shuʿbah narrated to us, from ʿĀṣim ibn ʿUbaydillah, who said I heard ʿAbdullāh ibn ʿĀmir ibn Rabīʿah, from his father that a woman from Banī Fazārah was married for (the dowry of) two sandals. The Messenger of Allah ﷺ said to her: 'Do you approve of (exchanging) yourself and your wealth for two sandals?' She said: 'Yes.' He said: "So he permitted it."[76]

76 al-Tirmidhī, *k. al-nikāḥ ʿan rasūlillah* ﷺ, *b. mā jāʾa fī muhūr al-nisāʾa*, 1113

12

TYPES OF WEAK AHADITH

As mentioned earlier, the scholars of ḥadīth have classified weak aḥādīth into several different categories based on the cause and type of weakness. These categories have been given very specific names or terms that tell us exactly what type of weakness is found in the narration. There are two primary causes for weakness in a narration:

1. a break in the chain of narrators
2. or a deficiency in the narrators

WEAK NARRATIONS BECAUSE OF A BREAK IN THE CHAIN OF NARRATORS

In Arabic the scholars of ḥadīth describe this category as المردود بسبب سقط من الإسناد, or weak narrations because of a gap in the chain of narrators. What is meant by a gap or break is that one narrator or more is missing from the isnād (chain), at any point in the chain, be it at the beginning, middle, or end. This gap could have been created intentionally or unintentionally and it can also be apparent or hidden. Basically, there is a narrator missing from the chain somewhere.

Based on where the narrator is dropped from the chain or how many are dropped from the chain the scholars of ḥadīth classify weak narrations into five categories:

1. Muʿallaq (Hanging)
2. Mursal (Loose)
3. Muʿḍal (Perplexing)
4. Munqaṭiʿ (Interrupted)
5. Mudallas (Hidden Defect)

AL-MUʿALLAQ (THE HANGING)

Linguistically, the word muʿallaq is the passive participle from the verb ʿallaqa (علّق), which means to hang, be suspended, dangle, cling, or adhere. The word muʿallaq literally means something that is hanging or dangling. Technically, al-Muʿallaq is a narration in which one or more narrators is dropped (omitted) from the beginning of the chain in sequence.

ما حذف من مبدأ إسناده راو فأكثر على التوالى

That is why it is called muʿallaq; it is literally as if the ḥadīth is hanging from the top. What is meant by the beginning of the chain is the narrator closest in time, or the teacher of the compiler. The end of the chain would be the Prophet ﷺ or the Companion ؓ. A person might omit the entire chain of narrators from beginning to end only quoting the Prophet ﷺ. For example, they may say the Prophet ﷺ said such and such. Or they may omit the entire chain of narrators except for the Companion or the Successor.

Example:

ما أخرجه البخارى فى مقدمة باب ما يذكر فى الفخذ، "وقال أبو موسى غطى النبى ﷺ ركبتيه حين دخل عثمان

At the beginning of the chapter on what has been narrated regarding the thighs being part of the ʿawrah, Imām al-Bukhārī ؒ brings a muʿallaq ḥadīth. He said, "Abū Mūsā ؓ said, 'The Prophet ﷺ covered his knees when ʿUthmān ؓ entered the room.'"

This particular narration is classified as muʿallaq because Imām al-

Bukhārī dropped the entire chain except for the Companion, Abū Mūsā al-Ashʿarī. The authenticity or strength of a muʿallaq narration depends on its chain of narrators. So just because a ḥadīth is muʿallaq does not automatically mean the ḥadīth is weak because oftentimes the chain of narrators is omitted or dropped for brevity. Imām al-Bukhārī has included a number of muʿallaq narrations in his collection as parts of chapter headings.

AL-MURSAL

Linguistically, the word mursal is the passive participle from the verb arsala (أرسل), which means to release, loosen, set free, or to send. So the word mursal literally means something that has been released, loosened, set free, or sent. Technically, a mursal narration is defined as a ḥadīth in which the companion narrator has been dropped or omitted from the chain.

هو ما سقط من آخر إسناده من بعد التابعي

Meaning, it is a ḥadīth in which the narrator is missing from the end of the chain, the one after the Tābiʿī, which is the companion narrator. Basically, a Successor reports the ḥadīth directly from the Prophet ﷺ without mentioning the Companion who they learned it from.

Example:

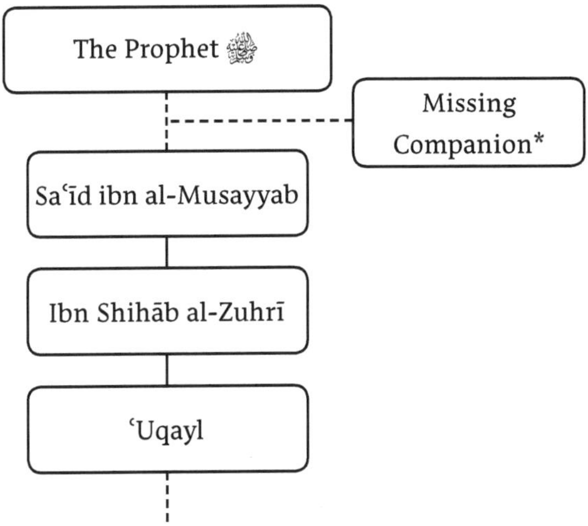

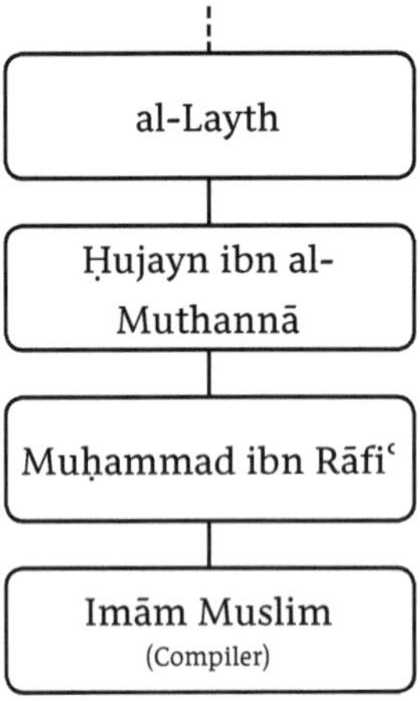

وَحَدَّثَنِي مُحَمَّدُ بْنُ رَافِعٍ، حَدَّثَنَا حُجَيْنُ بْنُ الْمُثَنَّى، حَدَّثَنَا اللَّيْثُ،
عَنْ عُقَيْلٍ، عَنِ ابْنِ شِهَابٍ، عَنْ سَعِيدِ بْنِ الْمُسَيَّبِ، أَنَّ رَسُولَ اللَّهِ
صلى الله عليه وسلم نَهَى عَنْ بَيْعِ الْمُزَابَنَةِ وَالْمُحَاقَلَةِ وَالْمُزَابَنَةُ
أَنْ يُبَاعَ ثَمَرُ النَّخْلِ بِالتَّمْرِ وَالْمُحَاقَلَةُ أَنْ يُبَاعَ الزَّرْعُ بِالْقَمْحِ
وَاسْتِكْرَاءُ الأَرْضِ بِالْقَمْحِ

Muḥammad ibn Rāfiʿ narrated to me, who said Ḥujayn ibn al-Muthanna narrated to us, who said al-Layth narrated to us, from ʿUqayl, from ibn Shihāb, from Saʿīd ibn al-Musayyab, who reported that the Messenger of Allah ﷺ forbade the transaction of al-Muzābanah and al-Muḥāqalah. al-Muzābanah means that fresh dates on the trees should be sold against dry dates. al-Muḥāqalah implies that the wheat in the ear should be sold against the wheat and getting the land on rent for the wheat (produced in it).[77]

This ḥadīth is classified as mursal because Saʿīd ibn al-Musayyab is from amongst the Successors. He passed away in the year 94. In this ḥadīth he is narrating directly from the Prophet ﷺ without mentioning the companion whom he heard it from. Now there is a lot of discussion amongst the scholars of ḥadīth regarding the authenticity of mursal narrations.

The mursal ḥadīth is initially classified as weak because there is a break in the chain of narrators. That missing link can be a Companion or it could

77 Muslim, *k. al-buyūʿ*, *b. taḥrīm bayʿ al-ruṭab bi al-tamr illa fī al-ʿarāyā*, 1539

be another tābʿī who can be strong or weak. There are multiple possibilities; there is only one narrator missing, which is the companion, or there could be more.

There are three major opinions regarding using a mursal ḥadīth as a legal proof:

1. The majority of ḥadīth scholars, jurists, and scholars of uṣūl are of the opinion that a mursal ḥadīth is weak and can not be used as a legal proof because the missing narrator is not known.
2. According to Imām Abū Ḥanīfah, Imām Mālik, and Imām Aḥmad a mursal ḥadīth is acceptable as long as the successor is known to be trustworthy who only narrates from other trustworthy sources.
3. Imām al-Shāfiʿī (ﷺ) was of the opinion that a mursal ḥadīth can be used as a valid legal proof as long as it meets certain conditions.

The discussion regarding the above mentioned conditions are beyond the scope of this short booklet. It is enough to know that mursal aḥādīth are accepted and acted upon as long as they meet certain conditions.

MURSAL AL-ṢAḤĀBĪ (THE MURSAL NARRATION OF A COMPANION)

A mursal ḥadīth of a Companion is when the Companion narrates something from the Prophet ﷺ that they did not hear or see themselves directly. This happened either because the Companion was extremely young during the life of the Prophet ﷺ or because they accepted Islam much later on and spent very little time with the Prophet ﷺ. There is almost unanimous agreement that the mursal ḥadīth of a Companion is authentic and a valid legal proof. This is because all of the Companions of the Prophet ﷺ are considered to be upright and accurate.

AL-MUʿḌAL

Linguistically, the word muʿḍal is the passive participle from the verb aʿḍala (أعضل), which means to become problematic, puzzling or mysterious. The word muʿḍal literally means something that is problematic, puzzling, or mysterious. Technically, a muʿḍal ḥadīth is a narration in which two or more narrators are missing from the chain in succession.

ما سقط من إسناده اثنان فأكثر على التوالى

It is called muʿḍal because the two or more missing narrators make the report mysterious.

Example:

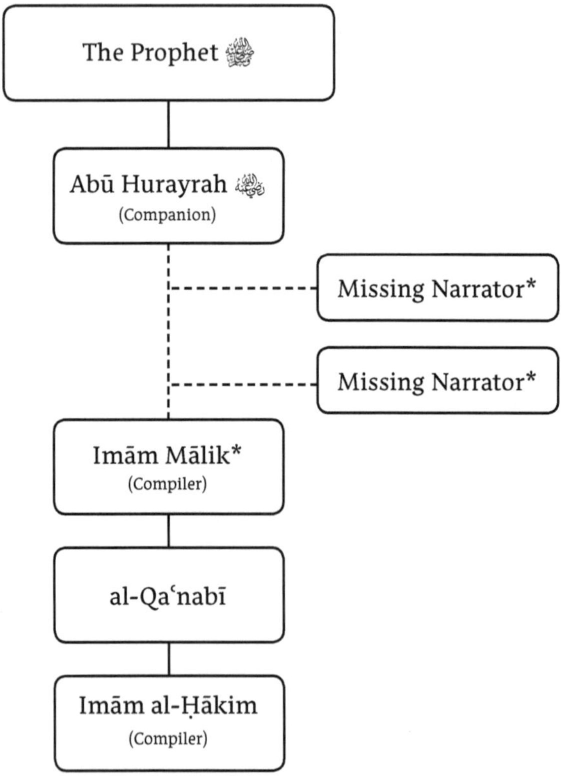

ما رواه الحاكم فى "معرفة علوم الحديث" بسنده إلى القعنبى عن مالك أنه بلغه أن أبا هريرة قال، قال رسول الله ﷺ للمملوك طعامه و كسوته بالمعروف و لا يكلف من العمل إلا ما يطيق

Imām Ḥākim narrates with his sanad till al-Qaʿnabī, from Mālik who narrated from Abū Hurayrah رضي الله عنه, who said that the Messenger of Allah ﷺ

said, "A slave is entitled to good food and clothes and should not be burdened with work they can't do."

This narration is classified as muʿḍal because there is no way Imām Mālik could've narrated this ḥadīth directly from Abū Hurayrah ﷺ. There is nearly a 40 year gap between them. Also, Imām Mālik's student, al-Qaʿnabī says "it reached him [Imām Mālik] that Abū Hurayrah said," which gives us insight that he didn't hear this directly from him. So it is known that there is at least one missing narrator for sure. However, when we study the entire corpus of ḥadīth, we find that there are two narrators missing between Imām Mālik and Abū Hurayrah ﷺ. From other sources, we find that Imām Mālik actually reported this ḥadīth from Muḥammad ibn ʿAjlān, from his father who then narrated it from Abū Hurayrah ﷺ.

AL-MUNQAṬIʿ

Linguistically, the word munqaṭiʿ is the active participle from the verb inqaṭaʿa (انقطع), which means to cut, sever or interrupt. The word munqaṭiʿ literally means something that is cut, severed or interrupted. Technically, a munqaṭiʿ narration is a ḥadīth that has a break anywhere in the chain.

ما لم يتصل إسناده على أى وجه كان انقطاعه

It is a narration that has a missing link or links somewhere in the chain of narrators. Meaning the missing link can be at the beginning, middle or end so this term is very general; it includes all the categories discussed above.

Example:

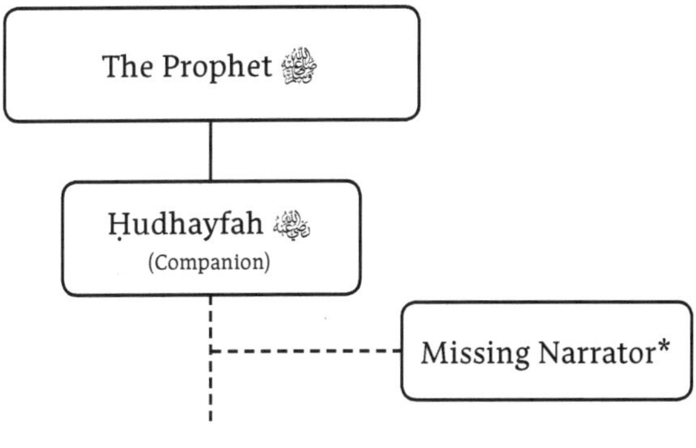

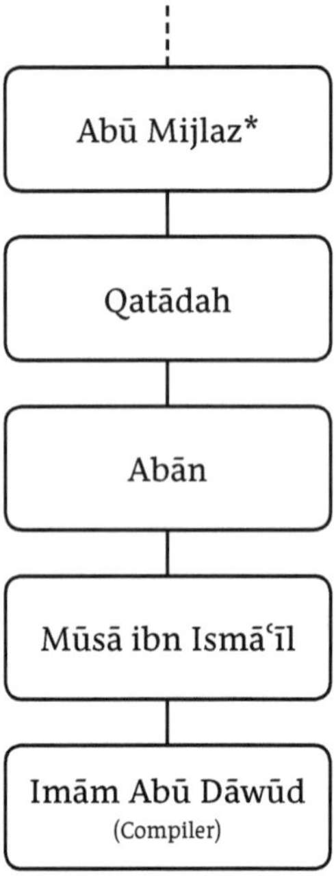

حَدَّثَنَا مُوسَى بْنُ إِسْمَاعِيلَ، حَدَّثَنَا أَبَانُ، حَدَّثَنَا قَتَادَةُ، قَالَ حَدَّثَنِي
أَبُو مِجْلَزٍ، عَنْ حُذَيْفَةَ، أَنَّ رَسُولَ اللَّهِ صلى الله عليه وسلم لَعَنَ
مَنْ جَلَسَ وَسْطَ الْحَلْقَةِ

Mūsā ibn Ismāʿīl narrated to us, who said that Abān narrated to us, who said that Qatādah narrated to us, who said that Abū Mijlaz narrated to me from Ḥudhayfah that the Messenger of Allah cursed the one who sat in the middle of a circle.[78]

The reason why this ḥadīth is classified as munqaṭiʿ is because there is a link missing between Abū Mijlaz and Ḥudhayfah. Abū Mijlaz is from the successors and he even met some of the companions but he never met Ḥudhayfah ibn al-Yamān. So there is definitely a link missing in between them.

AL-MUDALLAS

Linguistically, the word mudallas is the passive participle from the verb

78 Abū Dāwūd, *k. al-adab, b. al-julūs wasṭ al-ḥalqah*, 4826

dallasa (دلّس), which means to conceal. Tadlīs, literally, is concealing a defect in an object of sale from the buyer. Technically, a mudallas ḥadīth is a narration in which a defect in the chain of narrators is hidden (concealed) in order to make it look sound apparently.

إخفاء عيب فى الإسناد و تحسين لظاهره

A narrator conceals a defect in the chain, which is a missing link in order to make it seem as if the chain is free from any defects.

When a person does tadlīs they claim to narrate from their teacher, whom they met and learned from, that which they did not hear from them. For example, a narrator may narrate a ḥadīth on the authority of their teacher, but, the specific ḥadīth was not learnt directly from the teacher, but possibly from another student of the same teacher. At the time of the narration the narrator uses language that implies they learnt it directly from the teacher. Or they narrate from a contemporary of theirs whom they did not meet, in such a way to create the impression that they heard the ḥadīth from them directly.

WEAKNESS OF AHADITH DUE TO DEFICIENCIES IN THE NARRATORS

The second major reason for classifying aḥādīth as weak is because of some sort of deficiency or weakness in the narrator. In order for a ḥadīth to be classified as authentic all the narrators in the chain must be graded as upright and accurate. If there is any type of deficiency in either the uprightness or accuracy of one or more of the narrators then the narration is automatically graded as weak.

The scholars of ḥadīth have identified ten factors that are considered as deficiencies in a narrator; five are associated with uprightness and five are associated with accuracy. The five that are associated with uprightness are:

1. Lying (al-Kidhb)
2. Being Accused of lying (al-Ittihām bi al-Kidhb)
3. Open Sin (Fisq)
4. Being Unknown (Jahālah)

5. Innovation (bidʿah)

The five that are associated with accuracy are:

1. Neglect/Oversight (Ghaflah)
2. Frequent Errors (Fuḥsh al-Ghalaṭ)
3. Disagreement with Reliable Authorities and Narrators (Mukhālafah al-Thiqāt)
4. Misunderstandings (Kathrah al-Awhām)
5. Bad Memory (Sūʾ al-Ḥifdh)

Based on these ten factors the scholars of ḥādīth have classified aḥādīth into several different categories.

AL-MAWḌŪʿ

Linguistically, the word mawḍūʿ is the passive participle from the verb waḍaʿa (وضع), which means to place, lay down, or to invent. The word mawḍūʿ literally means something that has been placed or invented. Technically, a mawḍūʿ ḥadīth is a narration that has been fabricated. It is defined as a report made up by a liar that is attributed to the Prophet ﷺ.

هو الكذب المختلق المصنوع المنسوب إلى رسول الله ﷺ

One or more of the narrators in the chain was a known liar who was known to have told a lie upon the Prophet ﷺ. Not only is his uprightness deficient but it is non-existent.

This is the absolute worst type of narration. There is unanimous consensus amongst the scholars that it is not permissible to narrate a fabricated ḥadīth without saying or clarifying that it is fabricated.

AL-MATRŪK

Linguistically, the word matrūk is the passive participle from the verb taraka (ترك), which means to leave or abandon. The word matrūk literally means something that has been left, discarded, or abandoned. Technically, a matrūk ḥadīth is a narration in which one of the narrators has been accused of lying.

هو الحديث الذى فى إسناده راو متهم بالكذب

Meaning, the narrator is known to have a habit of lying even though it has not been explicitly proven that he or she ever lied regarding the Prophet ﷺ.

Example:

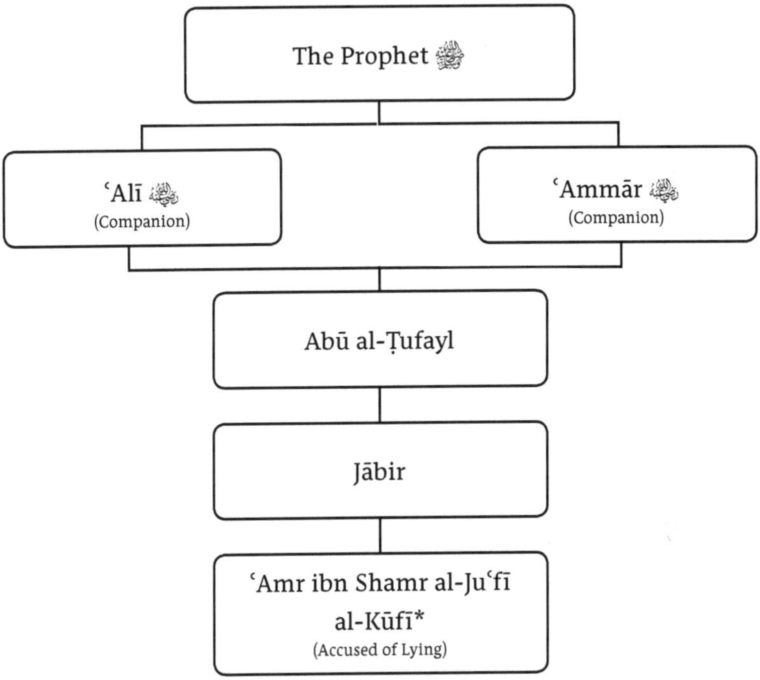

حديث عمرو بن شمر الجعفى الكوفى عن جابر عن أبى الطفيل
عن على وعمار قالا: كان النبى ﷺ يقنت فى الفجر ويكبر يوم
عرفة من صلاة الغداة ويقطع صلاة العصر آخر أيام التشريق

The ḥadīth of ʿAmr ibn Shamr al-Juʿfī al-Kūfī, from Jābir, from Abī al-Ṭufayl, from ʿAli and ʿAmmār who said that the Prophet ﷺ used to recite the qunūt in fajr and he would start the takbīr from the dawn of the day of ʿArafah and stop at ʿaṣr prayer on the last day of tashrīq.

Both Imām al-Nasāʾī and al-Dāraquṭnī commented that ʿAmr ibn Shamr is matrūk al-ḥadīth.

AL-MUNKAR

Linguistically, the word munkar is the passive participle of the verb ankara (أنكر), which means to reject, deny, rebuke, or criticize. The word munkar literally means something that has been rejected, denied, or criticized. Technically, a munkar ḥadīth has been defined in two different ways. The first definition given is that it is a narration whose chain contains a narrator who makes excessive mistakes (fuḥsh al-ghalaṭ), is extremely inattentive (ghaflah), or sins openly (fisq).

هو الحديث الذى فى إسناده راو فحش غلطه أو كثرت غفلته أو
ظهر فسقه

The second definition given is that it is a narration reported by a weak narrator that contradicts the narration of a reliable narrator.

هو ما رواه الضعيف مخالفا لما رواه الثقة

Examples:

An example of the first definition is the following ḥadīth recorded in al-Nasāʾī and Ibn Mājah:

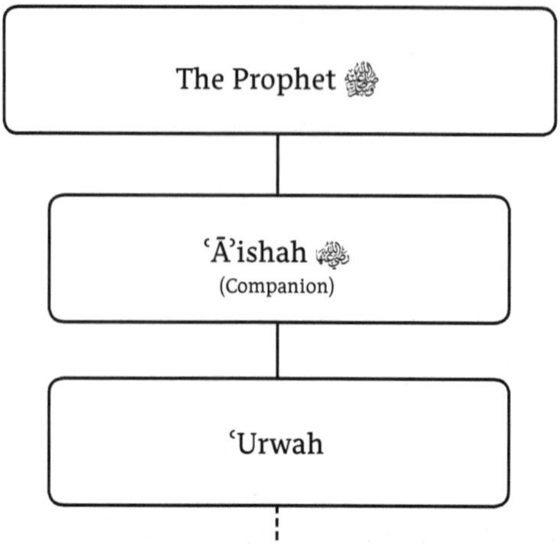

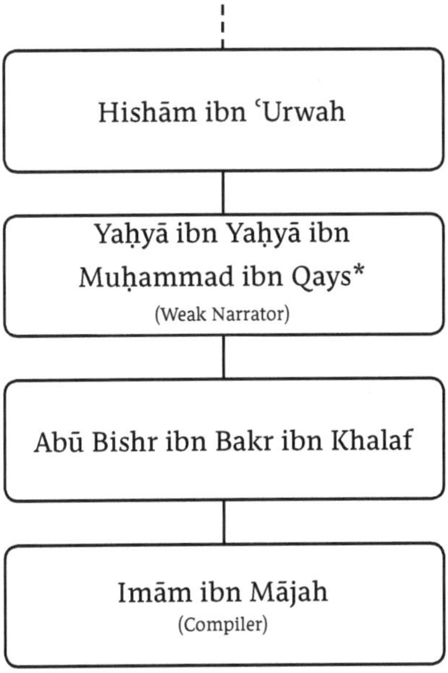

Abū Bishr ibn Bakr ibn Khalaf, from Yaḥyā ibn Yaḥyā ibn Muḥammad ibn Qays al-Madanī, from Hishām ibn ʿUrwah, from his father, from ʿĀʾishah, who reported the Prophet ﷺ saying, "Eat dried dates with the fresh ones, eat the new with the old for Satan turns angry and says, 'The son of Adam lives until he eats the old with the new .'"[79]

Imām al-Nasāʾī said, "This ḥadīth is munkar, because Yaḥyā ibn Yaḥyā ibn Muḥammad ibn Qays reported this ḥadīth by himself , though he is not in the position (in terms of retentiveness and accuracy) to report aḥādīth by himself."

An example of the second definition is the following ḥadīth recorded by Ibn Abī Ḥātim:

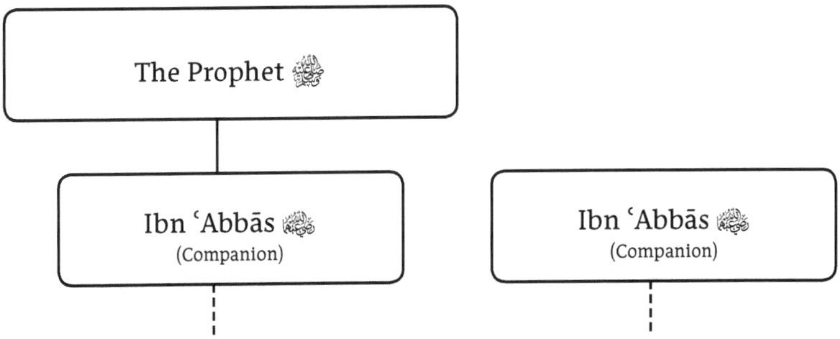

79 ibn Mājah, *k. al-aṭʿimah, b. akl al-balaḥ bi al-tamr*, 3330

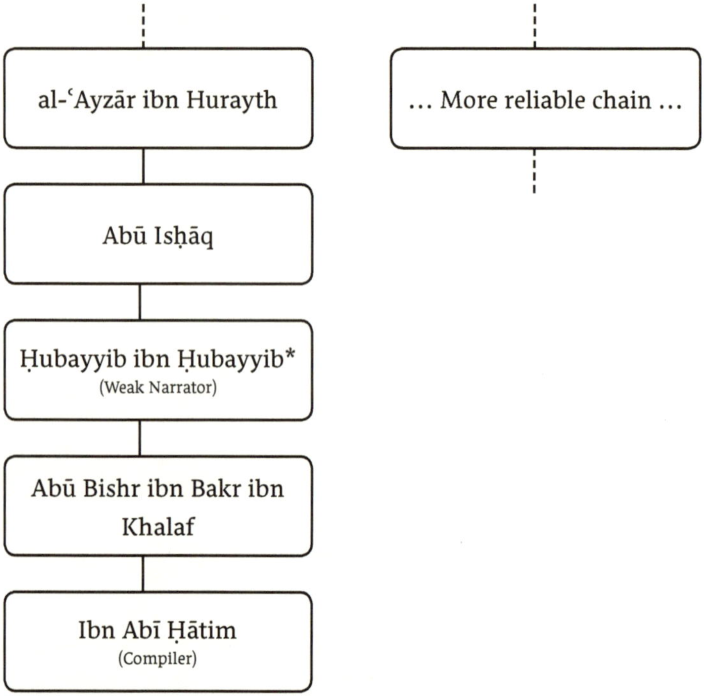

Ḥubayyib ibn Ḥubayyib, from Abū Isḥāq, from al-ʿAyzār ibn Hurayth, from ibn ʿAbbās ؓ, from the Prophet ﷺ who said, "Whoever establishes prayer, pays zakāh, performs ḥajj, fasts Ramaḍān and is generous to his guests will enter Paradise."

Ḥubayyib is graded as a weak narrator and his narration contradicts the report of another more reliable narrator who reported this ḥadīth as mawqūf upon ibn ʿAbbās ؓ. The version of the narration that is reported by a more reliable narrator is call maʿrūf . A maʿrūf ḥadīth is defined as what a reliable narrator reports in contradiction to a weak narrator.

هو ما رواه الثقة مخالفا لما رواه الضعيف

AL-SHĀDH

Linguistically, the word shādh is the active participle from the verb shadhdha (شذّ), which means to be alone, separate, or isolated. The word shādh literally means something that is alone, isolated, peculiar, or anomalous. Technically, a shādh ḥadīth is defined as a narration reported by a reliable narrator in contradiction to a more reliable narrator.

هو ما رواه المقبول مخالفا لمن هو أولى منه

The contradiction could take place either in the chain (isnād) or the text (matn) itself. The narration of the more reliable narrator is termed al-maḥfūẓ. It is defined as the narration of the more reliable narrator in contradiction to the reliable narrator.

هو ما رواه الأوثق مخالفا لرواية الثقة

Example:

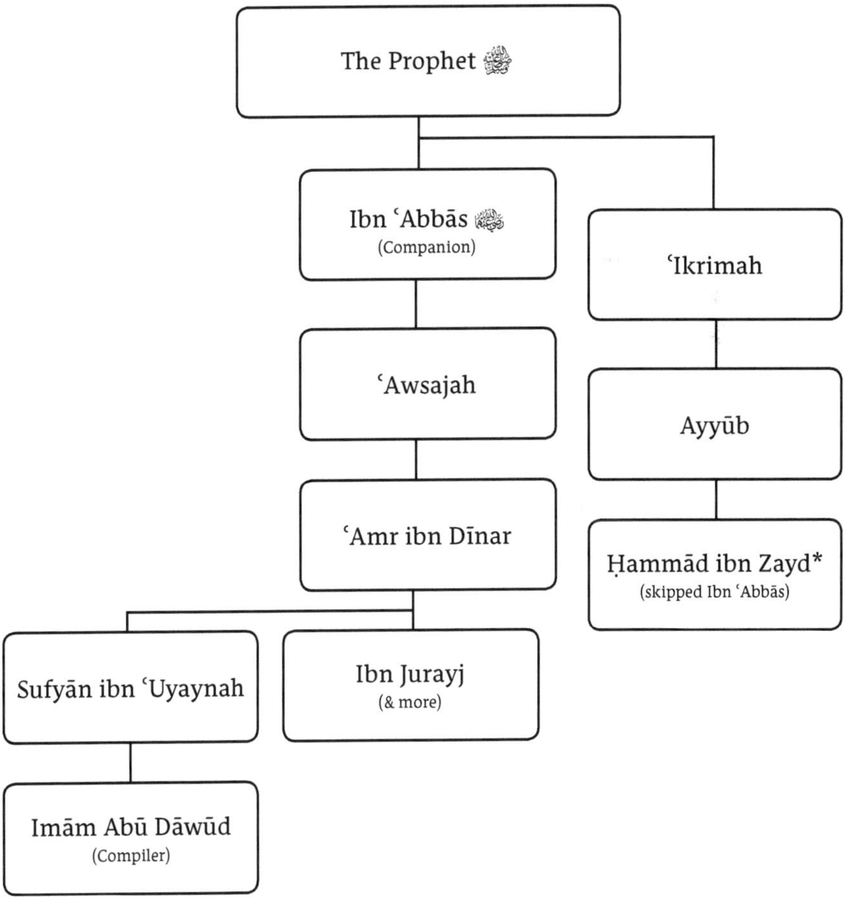

Ibn Abī ʿAmr, from Sufyān ibn ʿUyaynah, from ʿAmr ibn Dīnar, from ʿAwsajah, from ibn ʿAbbās ﷺ that a man died during the time of the Prophet ﷺ and did not leave any heirs except a freed slave. The Prophet ﷺ asked, "Did he leave anyone?" They replied, "No, except a slave whom he freed." So the Prophet ﷺ gave him all his inheritance.[80]

Sufyān ibn ʿUyaynah, Ibn Jurayj and others narrated this ḥadīth as uninterrupted (mawṣūl); whereas, Ḥammād ibn Zayd narrated it as mursal. Ḥammād is a reliable narrator, but his version is considered to be shādh because it contradicts the version of narrators who are more reliable.

AL-MUʿALLAL

Linguistically, the word muʿallal is the passive participle from the verb aʿalla (أعل), which means to make something defective, weak or to make an excuse. Technically, a muʿallal ḥadīth is defined as a narration with a hidden defect that affects its authenticity although it apparently seems to be authentic.

هو الحديث الذى اطلع فيه على علة تقدح فى صحته مع أن
الظاهر السلامة منها

It is a ḥadīth with a hidden defect that causes it to become weak. The hidden defect can sometimes be in the chain of the ḥadīth or in the text. An example of a hidden defect in the chain would be that there are two individuals, a student and his teacher, that lived during the same time period and it is an established fact that the student heard aḥādīth directly from the teacher. But after further investigation it becomes known that the student did not hear this particular ḥadīth directly from the teacher, but heard it from another student. Apparently the chain seems connected, but in reality there is a missing link.

Example:

Yaʿlā ibn ʿUbayd, from Sufyān al-Thawrī, from ʿAmr ibn Dīnār, from ʿAbdullah ibn ʿUmar, from the Prophet ﷺ who said, "Both parties have the option."

---

80 Abū Dāwūd, *k. al-farāʾiḍ*, 2905

The chain of this ḥadīth is connected and all of the narrators are graded as trustworthy and reliable. Apparently it seems to be sound and authentic. However, Yaʿlā ibn ʿUbayd made a mistake and mentioned the name ʿAmr ibn Dīnār, while the narration is actually from ʿAbdullāh ibn Dīnār.

AL-MUDRAJ

Linguistically, the word mudraj is the passive participle from the verb adraja (أدرج), which means to insert, include, or incorporate. Mudraj literally means something that has been inserted or included. Technically, a mudraj ḥadīth is defined as a narration whose chain has been mentioned incorrectly or a narration whose text has had something extra inserted into it.

ما غير سياق إسناده، أو أدخل في متنه ما ليس منه بلا فصل

Example:

ما رواه الخطيب من رواية أبي قطن و شبابة - فرقهما - عن شعبة عن محمد بن زياد عن أبي هريرة قال: قال رسول الله ﷺ أسبغوا الوضوء، ويل للأعقاب من النار

AL-MAQLŪB

Linguistically, the word maqlūb is the passive participle from the verb qalaba (قلب), which means to turn, turn inside out or outside in, upside down or invert. The word maqlūb literally means something that has been turned upside down or inside out. Technically, a maqlūb ḥadīth is defined as a narration in which one word has been replaced by another in the chain or text by reversing the order of the wording.

إبدال لفظ بآخر في سند الحديث أو متنه، بتقديم أو تأخير و نحوه

AL-MUḌṬARIB

Linguistically, the word muḍṭarib is the active participle from the verb iḍṭaraba (اضطرب), which means to be or become disorganized, disordered, disturbed, or restless. The word muḍṭarib literally means someone or something that makes something else disorganized, disordered, restless, or uneasy. Technically, a muḍṭarib ḥadīth is defined a narration that has been narrated in several different ways that are equal in strength.

ما روى على أوجه مختلفة متساوية فى القوة

Meaning there are discrepancies either in the chain, or text, or in both in each of the different versions of the ḥadīth that are difficult to reconcile because each version is of equal strength.

AL-MUṢAḤḤAF

Linguistically, the word muṣaḥḥaf is the passive participle from the verb ṣaḥḥafa (صحّف), which means to misplace the diacritical marks, to misread, mispronounce, or to distort. The words muṣaḥḥaf literally means something that has misplaced diacritical marks, is misread, mispronounced, or distorted. Technically, a muṣaḥḥaf ḥadīth is defined as a narration in which the orthography of the word is retained while the dots or vowels are changed.

تغيير الكلمة فى الحديث إلى غير ما رواه الثقات لفظا أو معنى

ACTING UPON AND USING WEAK NARRATIONS

Now a question that does arise is can weak aḥādīth be used? What is their legal value? Can they be used to derive or establish legal rulings? Can they be acted upon? Is it even permissible to narrate them?

The scholars of ḥadīth, uṣūl, and the jurists maintain that it is permissible to narrate weak aḥādīth with two conditions:

1. The ḥadīth should not be related to the field of belief or creed
2. The ḥadīth should not be associated with legal rulings

Based on the above two conditions, the majority of scholars are of the opinion that it is permissible to narrate weak aḥādīth that are related to virtuous deeds, encouraging good, discouraging evil, character, and stories.

However, when narrating a weak ḥadīth it should not be attributed directly to the Prophet ﷺ using definitive terms. Instead of using the expression "the Prophet ﷺ said such and such", one should say that "such and such was narrated about him or it has been narrated from him". The scholars use language that is in the passive voice.

When it comes to acting upon weak aḥādīth or using them as legal proofs there is unanimous agreement that it is not permissible to use weak aḥādīth for issues related to belief or creed. The vast majority also agree that it is not permissible to use weak aḥādīth to establish legal rulings. There is a disagreement amongst the scholars regarding the usage of weak aḥādīth related to the virtues or rewards of deeds, faḍā'il al-aʿmāl.

There are basically three major opinions when it comes to using weak aḥādīth for faḍā'il al-aʿmāl.

1. Weak aḥādīth should not be acted upon without exception, regardless of whether they are in beliefs, legal rulings, encouraging and warning or righteous deeds. This was the opinion of great ḥadīth scholars such as, Yaḥyā ibn Maʿīn, al-Bukhārī, Muslim, ibn al-ʿArabī the scholar of the Mālikīs, Abu Shama al-Muqaddasi from the scholars of the Shafiʿī's, and Ibn Ḥazm.
2. It is permissible to act upon weak aḥādīth without exception if there is nothing else related in that area of discussion. This was the opinion of Abū Ḥanīfah, al-Shāfiʿī, Mālik, and Aḥmad ibn Ḥanbal.
3. It is permissible to act upon weak aḥādīth that are related to fadā'il al-aʿmāl, al-targhīb and al-tarhīb, and not those that are related to beliefs and legal rulings.

It is important to note that the scholars who permitted the use of weak aḥādīth for virtues and to promote good and warn against evil did not leave the door wide open to allow citing every single weak ḥadīth. Rather, they placed three conditions that regulate the use of weak ḥadīth:

1. That the ḥadīth not be very weak. Basically, it should not be a fabricated ḥadīth.
2. That the ḥadīth be within the scope of an authentic legal principle that is applied and accepted in either the Quran or Sunnah.
3. That its weakness, not authenticity, be realized when applying it.

> What that means is that when acting upon it a person should not believe with full certainty that the Prophet ﷺ himself actually said it or did it. Rather, there is a possibility he did so and it is being acted upon in hope of receiving reward.

No scholar permitted the narration and use of weak aḥādīth indiscriminately, but rather, stipulated the conditions mentioned above.

FURTHER READING

ENGLISH WORKS

- Kamali, Mohammad Hashim. A Textbook of Ḥadīth Studies. Leicestershire, UK: The Islamic Foundation, 2009
- Azami, Muhammad Mustafa. Studies in Hadīth Methodology and Literature. USA: American Trust Publications, 2012
- Brown, Jonathan A.C. Hadith Muhammad's Legacy in the Medieval and Modern World. UK: Oneworld Publications, 2010

ARABIC WORKS

- ʿItr, Nūr al-Dīn. Manhaj al-Naqd fī ʿUlūm al-Ḥadīth. Damascus: Dār al-Fikr, 2006
- Al-Ṭaḥḥān, Maḥmūd. Taysīr Muṣṭalaḥ al-Ḥadīth. Karachi: Maktabah al-Bushrā, 2014

BIBLIOGRAPHY

- al-Bukhārī, Muḥammad b. Ismāʿīl. Al-Jāmiʿ al-Ṣaḥīḥ . Cited by chapter, subchapter system.
- b. al-Ḥajjāj, Muslim. Ṣaḥīḥ Muslim. Cited by chapter, subchapter system.
- al-Nasāʾī, Aḥmad b. Shuʿayb. Sunan. Cited by chapter, subchapter system.
- al-Sijistānī, Abū Dāwūd. Al-Sunan. Cited by chapter, subchapter system.
- al-Tirmidhī, Muḥammad b. ʿĪsā. Al-Jāmiʿ. Cited by chapter, subchapter system.
- al-Haythami, ʿAlī b. Abū Bakr. Majmaʿ al-Zawāʾid. Cited by chapter, subchapter system.
- al-Ḥākim, Muḥammad b. ʿAbdullah al-Naysāburī. Al-Mustadrak ʿalā al-Ṣaḥiḥayn.

ABOUT THE AUTHOR

Shaykh Furhan Zubairi was born in 1983 in Indianapolis, IN. Shortly thereafter, he moved and spent most of his youth in Southern California, graduating from high school in Irvine in 2001. He began his pursuit of Islamic knowledge and spirituality at the Institute of Knowledge (IOK) in 1998 where he started the memorization of the Quran and studied the primary books in the Islamic sciences and Arabic language. After starting college, he took a break and went to Karachi, Pakistan for 9 months to complete the memorization of the Quran at Jamiʿah Binoria. He returned home and completed his B.S. in Biological Sciences from the University of California, Irvine in 2005. He then traveled to Egypt to further his studies of the Arabic language. Thereafter, his pursuit of Islamic knowledge led him back to Pakistan where he completed a formal 'Alamiyyah degree (Masters in Arabic and Islamic Studies) at the famous Jami'ah Darul-Uloom in Karachi, where he studied with prominent scholars. He has obtained numerous ijaazaat (traditional licenses) in the six authentic books of hadith Siha Sittah as well as the Muwattas of Imam Malik and Imam Muhammad and has also received certification in the field of Islamic Finance. Shaykh Furhan Zubairi serves as the Director of Religious Education and is the Dean of the Seminary Program (IOKseminary.com) at the Institute of Knowledge in Diamond Bar, CA. He regularly delivers khutbahs and lectures at various Islamic Centers and events in Southern California.

The Institute of Knowledge Seminary Curriculum Series is a collection of books designed to build literacy amongst the Muslim community in the major branches of Islamic Studies including ʿAqīdah, Quran, Ḥadīth, Fiqh, Uṣūl al-Fiqh, Sīrah and Tazkiyah. The books go hand in hand with the with the courses offered through the IOK Seminary Program, which provides educational courses, programs and seminars to the wider local and international community.

Visit **IOKseminary.com** to learn more, view the full catalog and attend classes on-site, online and on-demand.

FORTHCOMING WORKS:

- A Brief Introduction to Uṣūl al-Fiqh
- A Brief Introduction to Tajwīd
- A Brief Commentary on Imām al-Nawawī's Forty Ḥadīth
- Tafsīr of Juz ʿAmma
- An Introduction to the Ḥanafī Madhab

NOTES

NOTES

NOTES

Made in the USA
Las Vegas, NV
29 August 2024

94554322R00088